Y0-BDA-803

K.W.
2018

TV OR NO TV?

A Primer on the Psychology of Television

Faye B. Steuer
Jason T. Hustedt

The Robert Arthur Williams Library
Florida Hospital College of Health Sciences
800 Lake Estelle Drive
Orlando, Florida 32803

University Press of America,® Inc.
Lanham · New York · Oxford

HQ
784
·T4
S84
2002

Copyright © 2002 by
University Press of America,® Inc.
4720 Boston Way
Lanham, Maryland 20706
UPA Acquisitions Department (301) 459-3366

PO Box 317
Oxford
OX2 9RU, UK

All rights reserved
Printed in the United States of America
British Library Cataloging in Publication Information Available

ISBN 0-7618-2433-2 (paperback : alk. ppr.)

⊖™ The paper used in this publication meets the minimum
requirements of American National Standard for Information
Sciences—Permanence of Paper for Printed Library Materials,
ANSI Z39.48—1984

To the four no-TV families,
who generously shared their
thoughts and experiences

Contents

Preface

Very few North American families raise their children without television. In fact, 99% of U.S. families with children under the age of 18 have at least one television set in their homes. The 1% who do not are a disparate and little-studied group. In all likelihood, they include both those whose TV-less status is temporary and those who will live without television for many years. Some of them may not own a set because of economic or other practical considerations while others have made a conscious decision to minimize the influence of television in their lives.

This book grew out of a study of four families who have lived for several years without television and have done so not because of practical necessity but because their adult members actively wish to avoid the influences of television while raising children. We were interested in such families in part because the first author grew up during a time when no U.S. families owned television sets. Later, when raising her own child, she was impressed by the many ways in which TV insinuates itself into family life. Simultaneously, her brother and sister-in-law opted not to own a television for the first 13 years of their daughter's life. The first author thus had the repeated opportunity to observe, first-hand, a no-TV family in a TV world. What she saw was conversation, reading, friendships, civic engagement, the making of music, and the pursuing of hobbies—nothing, in short, that would be cause for alarm. And yet her brother's family often came under pressure from friends and family to get a television set.

When we conceived the current study in 1995, we wondered if we would be able to find *any* families who had children younger than 18 but did not have television. We decided to run an advertisement in the local Sunday paper to see if we could discover one or more such families. When we inquired about placing the advertisement, the person we talked to volunteered the opinion that we would not be able to find any families of the type we were looking for. Even though we feared he might be right, we ran the ad anyway and, eventually, located the four families whose experiences form the basis for this book.

We treated each family as a separate case study, eliciting several types of information from the members of each. Later, as we studied the opinions and experiences they shared with us, we discovered six common themes that characterize the beliefs of all four families. In Chapters 2 through 7, we examine scientific evidence that addresses the six beliefs of the no-TV families. These relate to the time devoted to television in TV households, the content of television shows (i.e., sex and aggression), addiction to television, television's influence on thinking, television and reading, and the influences of television advertising. In addition, a superordinate theme—television's influence on children's development of *inner resources*—touches upon each of the other six themes and is discussed in Chapter 8.

This is a book, then, that presents the no-TV experience through the eyes of the four families we studied. It is also a primer on the psychological effects of television as revealed by scientific investigations that have been conducted over the last several decades.

We have written the book at a level suitable for use as a supplementary reader in undergraduate psychology and communications courses. We think it will be of interest to people in many disciplines who wonder about the lasting effects of television and who want a succinct introduction to scientific research on the topic.

Acknowledgments

We offer our profuse thanks, first of all, to the four anonymous families who generously shared their time and their unique knowledge with us. Without them, this book never would have come into being.

We thank, too, Merillat Staat Saint-Amand, Will Moody, and Kristin Yohler, all of whom were students at the College of Charleston during the time they participated in this project. Merillat and Will took part in interviews and created transcripts of interviews. Kristin also created transcripts. All three worked cheerfully, tirelessly, and accurately and we are most grateful for their help.

We are grateful to Drs. James Hittner and Jerome Singer, who read and made comments on earlier drafts of the manuscript. Although we accept full responsibility for the final product, we feel most fortunate to have had the benefit of their insights.

Chapter 1

Introduction

This book was inspired by four families who are raising their children without television. None of these families has a TV set anyplace in the home. In studying them, we employed a case study methodology, treating each family as a single case. As we undertook this work, we discovered that families who do not have television and who do have children under the age of 18 are quite rare. In two years, we were able to find only four families who fit this description, were willing to be interviewed, and were within driving distance of our base of operations.

None of our no-TV families know each other. Parents in each family arrived at the decision not to have television independently. The families differ in terms of the ages of the parents, ages of the children, educational training of the parents, parental occupations, religious beliefs, and the neighborhoods in which they live. Despite their differences, however, all four of the families raised a great many of the *same* issues when they talked with us about living without television. As we have studied the information and insights they shared, we have come to appreciate that they have in common a unique, outsider's understanding of the impact of television on contemporary children and families.

We have been surprised, as our readers may be, with the similarities among the observations made by the various parents in our studies. Each of Chapters 2 through 7 of this book focuses on a particular observation (or set of related observations) of the no-TV families regarding how they perceive television to influence families and growing children. We begin each of these chapters with quotations from questionnaires or interview responses of the no-TV parents. We then proceed to examine what the existing scientific literature has to say regarding their views. In many ways, then, this is a book *about* television. Its subject matter is organized around the common beliefs of the eight no-TV parents in our case studies.

Method of Study: General Considerations

It is typical in psychology to do studies that will permit us to make generalizations about our findings. To that end, we often study a sample of people who are representative of some larger group. However, such a strategy is only feasible when investigators know something about the larger group. If we can specify its key characteristics, then we can have a certain amount of confidence when it comes to sampling a subset of the group for intensive study. After data have been collected from the sample, we typically use statistical techniques to summarize the data and draw conclusions from them. When such studies are carefully planned and conducted, conclusions are likely to take the form of general statements about the larger group.

Such conditions do not readily apply in the case of families who do not have television sets. Little has been published and little is known about such families. We do know that, by early 1998, 99% of U.S. households that had a child or children under the age of 18 also had TV. This figure is an estimate provided by Nielsen Media Research, the well-known organization that rates television shows as to audience size (T. Dolson, personal communication, February 20, 1998). So only about 1% of U.S. families with children do not have television at the present time.

When we began planning our research on no-TV families we did not have even this much information. We knew only that 98.3% of U.S. households had at least one television set (U.S. Bureau of the Census, 1994) and we suspected that an even higher percentage of families with children would have TV. We suspected as well that television-less families would be a diverse group—probably including those who were temporarily without television because of a set malfunction or because the family was in the midst of a move, those who could not afford a TV, and those who, like the families we ultimately studied, actively wished not to have television in their homes.

When researchers sample from a group that exists in abundance —all fifth graders, say, or all working mothers over the age of 40—it is often relatively easy to identify the group and to come up with some sensible way to contact a subset of its members. Finding members of a very small group that may be prone to shifting membership, however, was a more difficult matter. Early on, we abandoned any attempt to find a representative sample of this group in favor of a more exploratory approach, which we felt was appropriate given the lack of research on contemporary families without television. First, we wanted to know if we could find *any* such families and then, if we could, we wanted to get to know them. We chose as our approach the case study method.

The Present Case Studies: Procedures

A case study involves examining a particular individual or group (in our case, a family) in detail. It may incorporate information gleaned from interviews, questionnaires, observations, archival information, or any combination thereof. Case studies are often appropriate when a new phenomenon is being investigated or when an especially rare or unique circumstance merits study (Abramson, 1992; Yin, 1994). Some use broader terms, such as *qualitative research* or *ethnographic research*, to refer to investigations that rest less on statistical analyses and more on verbal descriptions (Creswell, 1994; Lindlof & Meyer, 1998).

Our first task was to find out whether there were any no-TV families, with children, who lived close enough for us to get to know them. We ran an advertisement in a Sunday edition of our local newspaper, *The Charleston Post and Courier*, that read in part as follows:

We are interested in locating families who are raising
CHILDREN IN HOMES WITHOUT TELEVISION
If you are doing so and would be willing to be interviewed
as part of a research project...
please call...

The estimated Sunday circulation of the newspaper is in the neighborhood of 124,000. The ad resulted in calls from or regarding 13 families. Three of these families actually had TV sets in their homes (although they were used infrequently), three had children who were already grown, and four either got television or changed their minds about participating after the initial contact. The remaining three did have children, did not have television, and became participants in our study. Two years later, we ran the ad again and got only one call—from a family that had recently moved into the area. That family also qualified and participated in the study.

Our goal was to get the maximum amount of information in the minimum amount of time, so as not to unnecessarily inconvenience the busy families who agreed to share their experiences with us. After obtaining informed consent from the parents, we proceeded to gather information about them and their children in three successive phases:

1) Questionnaires were mailed to each participating family—one questionnaire for each family member. Parent questionnaires were quite lengthy (10 pages) and solicited information on ages of family members, education, occupation, history of television use, how the decision not to have TV came about, religion, disciplinary techniques used with children, satisfaction with the decision not to have television, activities and hobbies, accomplishments of self and spouse, reading habits and preferences, sources of news and information, whether they voted in the last election, radio preferences, movie attendance, and use of other technological devices and appliances. Three-page child questionnaires asked for information about age, school, grade, reading habits and preferences, participation in groups or teams, hobbies, lessons (such as music or dancing lessons), and favorite ways to spend free time. Questionnaires were returned to us and we then scheduled an interview.

2) In phase 2, one or both investigators interviewed each family in the home. When only one investigator was present, she was accompanied by research assistants who took notes and checked to be sure all planned questions were asked. All family members were present at the interviews. A series of open-ended questions focused on pressures or support the family has experienced as a result of not having television, extent of exposure to TV outside the home, children's satisfaction with the family's decision not to have television, academic achievement and peer relationships of the children, and amount of reading material available in the home. We also used the interviews to clear up any confusion we had after reading the questionnaire responses. Interviews took about 2 hours. We were, in every case, seated around the family's dining table. All families gave us permission to make audio tapes of the interviews. Before leaving the home, we distributed activity logs for family members to fill out.

3) In phase 3, participants were asked to complete an activity log for each family member over a 7-day period. The log was essentially a 24-hour time diary, marked off in 30-minute intervals, and enabled participants to show how they occupied their waking hours. They were instructed to designate their activities in quite general terms, such as "working," "sleeping,"

"doing chores," "reading," or "getting ready" (which connoted getting ready to go out or to bed). We asked them to omit mention of any activities they felt were of a personal nature. All four no-TV families completed phases 1 and 2; only three of the four returned their activity logs. Tapes of interviews were later transformed into typed transcripts, which were scrutinized by the investigators as well as subjected to a computer search for designated topics of conversation—"violence," for example, or "advertising." The software used for this purpose is called The Text Collector. It permits searches for words, parts of words, or combinations of words (O'Neill Software, 1995).

The method of data collection allowed us to establish a personal relationship with the no-TV families and to explore in detail their various experiences, thoughts, and feelings about television and about life without it. While interviews enabled us to concentrate our attention on the unique experiences and provocative insights of the families, the questionnaires provided basic information that permits us to place the families in the context of North American society generally. Let's look at the families.

The No-TV Families

Like any group of families, the no-TV families in our study are alike in some ways and different in others. We begin with some of their similarities and then move to a brief description of each family individually. First, it is obvious that none of these families is without television because of economic necessity. All have occupations or resources that place them in the middle or upper-middle class socially and economically. They are all intact families, which is to say that they all consist of two married parents and a set of children who belong to those two parents. All of the parents are very concerned with the experiences of their children and feel that provision of a television-free atmosphere in the home is of benefit to their offspring.

The spousal pairs agree at a very basic level on the decision not to have television and they have all lived without television at least since their oldest children were infants. None belongs to an organization that prohibits or discourages television ownership. Although they have strong feelings about television, none attempts to recruit others to the no-TV lifestyle. In fact, all mentioned that other people often seem to feel "defensive," "judged," or "indicted" regarding their *own* use of television when they hear about a family that does not have TV. So these families have all come to soft-pedal the television issue in many situations. All of the parents expressed the belief that they would not have *time* to watch TV even if they had it. They value reading and do it regularly, making frequent use of the public library. They spend time talking with each other and with their children. All of them listen to public radio and get their news from newspapers and radio. Both the adults and the children are occasionally exposed to TV outside the home —at other people's houses, in school, or elsewhere.

One is struck by the apparent health and normality of these families. The children are developing in homes where the parents are in agreement and in charge. The youngsters get a great deal of input and attention from their mothers and fathers and ample opportunity to explore their own creativity and resourcefulness. This should become apparent in the individual family descriptions that follow, in which names have been changed to protect study participants' anonymity.

The Fields. The Fields live in an attractive brick home surrounded by trees on a quiet, urban, residential street. The parents, Barbara (whose age we did not learn) and Nelson, 44, greeted us warmly and introduced us to their 15-year-old daughter, Cynthia, a tenth grader, and their 10-year-old son, Arthur, who is in fifth grade. Nelson Field has a high school education and sells real estate for a living. Barbara is a substitute teacher with a partial college education. Both of the children are excellent students and attend academic magnet schools. The Fields are the only Black family in our group.

Barbara and Nelson have not had a television set in the entire time (18 years) that they have been married. When they married they agreed that they wanted to spend their limited free time doing things other than watching television. This is a fact that they normally do not talk about, for they have learned that others may think the Fields are judging them if it comes out that they do not have TV. They will talk about their decision if somebody asks, but they do not bring up the subject. When we asked, they told us that they did not have time to waste watching television. And, as Barbara put it on her questionnaire, "We wanted our children to receive the maximum mental stimulation, family interaction, realistic values and expectations from life" and to "develop self-sufficiency." The content of many TV programs, she feels, undermines the moral values she and Nelson are trying to teach their children. Nelson noted during our interview that he believes television promotes materialism—something he does not want to cultivate in his children.

Barbara noted the value of silence and, indeed, we could hear a distant dog bark as we talked in their home on that spring evening. The Fields—all four of them—clearly value diligence, accomplishment, togetherness, and spirituality. They are Jehovah's Witnesses and all are active in their congregation of fellow worshipers. The family usually sits down to both breakfast and dinner together, with morning a favored time for family Bible reading. Both the children excel at school and spend significant time on both studies and hobbies. Cynthia shows a particular creative flair in sewing and jewelry-making. She showed us several dresses she had made and pointed out how she incorporated her own design features into some of the dress patterns. Arthur favors sports and reading and also collects stamps and pennies. The Field children appear to be emulating the example set by their industrious parents. Barbara makes silk flower arrangements for weddings and also plays the piano. Nelson helps the family with his talents for home and car repair.

The children find that by now all their friends know they do not have TV and they experience essentially no pressure or derision from classmates over this issue. Neither child anticipates having television later in life. As Cynthia puts it, "Once you get used to *doing* things, just sitting and watching is boring." Barbara reports that they all find what is on television to be "shocking," if they happen to see it while staying in a motel. She feels that "since we don't have television we are more sensitive to the things that are on." As to keeping up with the news, they rely on radio, the newspaper, and word of mouth. Nelson says, "It's sufficient to hear about it...you don't have to watch the atrocities."

The Greenwald Lakes. Eve Greenwald, 47, and Adam Lake, 54, have been married for 19 years and have a 14-year-old son, Isaac, and a 10-year-old daughter, Anna. Isaac is in eighth grade in public school. Anna attends fourth grade in a private school that provides special instruction for children with dyslexia. The Greenwald Lakes (like the two families yet to be described) are White. Eve was raised in France by American parents and Adam, also American, lived for several years in France.

We visited them at their home—a sturdy, welcoming structure in the country, surrounded by woods. Access to the house is by an unpaved road. Adam designed the home—with its high ceilings and numerous built-in bookcases—and he and Eve built it together, with some help from friends. Clearly, "home" to this family lies not just within the walls and roof of the house, but includes the surrounding woods and the garden that is tended by Eve.

Eve and Adam feel they are fortunate to have enough inheritance and trust fund resources that they do not have to work at regular, income-producing jobs. Their days are full of activities, however. Eve is a talented singer with a classical repertoire who devotes several hours a day to studying and practicing music. She also does origami, makes cards, walks, jogs, bikes, and does her gardening and landscaping. She has specialized training in carpentry. Adam has a Ph.D. in philosophy and spends much of his time writing poetry—often haiku—and working in his print shop, where he produces delicate hand-sewn books. At other times, he pursues interests in Zen Buddhism, boating, nature walking, and listening to music. Both Eve and Adam are devoted readers.

Both also spend a lot of time with their children—talking, playing games, doing homework and reading (especially with Anna), chauffeuring, and going on special outings and adventures. They all eat dinner together every night. Isaac's preferred out-of-school activities include reading, collecting various things (rocks, coins, stamps, bones, plants, and "out of the ordinary" things), day dreaming, and looking at catalogs. He lists day dreaming as his favorite thing to do in his free time and his mother confirms that this is a special passion of his. He too reads voraciously, having worked his way through all the children's classics at the local library before he was 12. He does well in school and will attend an academic magnet school next year. Anna takes piano lessons, enjoys bike riding, and particularly enjoys playing pretend games and card games. Both children socialize with friends regularly and both report that they have been teased at school for their family's being too "poor" to have TV. Isaac is adamant about wanting to be a 100% no-TV kid and does not plan to have television if he has children when he grows up. Anna feels less strongly than Isaac in this regard, but her mother reports that wanting TV is "not a big theme" with her.

Eve and Adam had television at various times early in their marriage but when Adam's teenaged son from a previous marriage—a native French speaker—stayed with them and overused television, the Greenwald Lakes gave their TV away. That occurred when Isaac was a baby, so neither he nor Anna remembers having TV in the home. Their parents feel that television is of poor quality "both intellectually and aesthetically," that it is boring, and that they do not have time for it. They are offended by the commercials and by the intrusive nature of the medium. Adam says, "I believe not having television has allowed my children to develop the inner resources to amuse themselves in manifold ways."

The Lotts. The Lotts are the largest of the families we studied. Ben and Laura Lott and their four children fill a substantial stone and frame urban home with activity and excitement. All of the children were adopted into the family as infants. Ben is a 40-year-old cardiologist and Laura, a 49-year-old, college-educated nurse-turned-homemaker. Their children are Michael, 13 and in eighth grade; Suzanne, an 11-year-old fifth grader; Bronwyn, age 8 and in third grade; and Eric who, at age 4, attends a church kindergarten on weekday mornings. The children are in both public and private schools.

With four children ranging from the teens to the preschool years, these parents keep very busy seeing to it that their youngsters arrive at schools and at their various activities on time. In addition to their parental enterprises, Ben and Laura keep full schedules of personal activities as well. Laura reads, actively supports political candidates, belongs to garden and book clubs, walks, is a board member at a women's shelter, and has served as president of the Parent Teacher Organization. Ben, in addition to the medical practice that occupies him from early morning until 6:30 PM (barring emergencies), plays piano, visits museums, runs, hikes, camps, roller blades, rock climbs, and enjoys spectator sports. The majority of these leisure activities he shares with various other members of the family. All of the Lotts are active in the Presbyterian church.

In addition to church groups and events, the three older children share an affinity for baseball and skiing. All three also take piano lessons. Michael and Suzanne roller blade. Michael lists skateboarding as one of his favorite leisure activities and he also plays soccer and goes rock climbing with his father. Suzanne most enjoys going skating, going to movies, and spending time with her friends. She also swims, plays basketball, and plays handbells and cello. She and Bronwyn both ride horses. Bronwyn says reading and baseball are her favorite pastimes. She is also a Brownie scout and plays the viola. She has the reputation in the family of being the child who most likes to read. At 4, Eric spends most of his time playing. He especially likes Lincoln logs and blocks. He rides a bike, is in a children's music group, and is read to and listens to audio books. Despite multiple busy schedules, the Lotts usually manage to sit down to dinner as a family two or three nights a week.

Laura and Ben have lived without television since they were married, 14 years ago. Both profess to be "addicted" to television and in order to assure that they would have time to interact with one another, they agreed from the beginning that it would be best not to have a TV in their home. According to Ben, this is a primary reason for continuing not to have television today. Laura and Ben believe, as well, that as a result of not having TV their children have better abilities to entertain themselves, read, and sustain attention to tasks. Laura notes that on occasions when they have rented a TV for a few days they "stop talking to each other."

When we asked about the reactions of others to their not having TV, Suzanne and Michael were quick to say that other children ask about it and Michael, in particular, would clearly rather his family had television. Suzanne is noncommittal on the subject. Bronwyn feels being without television is "okay" and is glad she is not addicted to it so she can play outside. Little Eric opines that it is "okay" too. Laura speculates that they all will have TV when they grow up.

Every stable family probably develops an ethos that characterizes its members and their interactions. The Lotts' ethos appears to be one of activity, athleticism, musicianship, and domestic organization.

The Stellings. We visited the Stellings in their modern home in a new suburban neighborhood. When we arrived Joellen, 34, and Carlton, 3, greeted us. Dave, 39, and Christina, 4, were en route back home after a trip to the library. Joellen is a full-time homemaker and mother with a partial college education. Dave is a college graduate whose occupation is selling insurance.

Like most of the other no-TV families, the Stellings have been without TV since they got married (5 years ago). In their case, the decision not to have television was spearheaded by Joellen, who feels that TV played a major role in the dissolution of her previous marriage. In that relationship, she reports, the constant operation of the television became a point of contention that could not be resolved. On his questionnaire, Dave succinctly summarized his role in this decision: "My wife didn't want one. I wanted her." He says that he vaguely missed the TV for a month or so, but came to fully embrace the no-TV decision, particularly in light of the benefits to his children.

The Stellings are busy establishing themselves in a new community, having moved from another state. Their activities at present tend to focus on home, family, and church. They are active Baptists. Joellen also pursues interests in reading, basket making, photography, painting, and water skiing. Dave enjoys gardening, reading, biking, swimming, running, wood working, and stamp collecting. Both are fans of stock car racing and they admit that every so often they miss watching the car races on TV. Christina likes to fish, swim, and ride her bike. She also belongs to a children's garden club. Carlton likes playing, bike riding, and fishing. Both children are very fond of being read to and their parents typically read to them at least 30 minutes a day. Joellen has read to them since they were young infants and believes that the stimulation of reading fostered their early facility with language. Both Cristina and Carlton can recite the Pledge of Allegiance from memory. Dave's office is nearby and he is home most of the time for both lunch and dinner, so the Stellings eat nearly all their meals together.

Like the other families, the Stellings get their news from radio and the newspaper. They prefer this to what they perceive as the violent and sensationalized television news. Joellen says, "I can read the [newspaper] headlines and know that I don't have to go any further down in that article than the headlines. 'Two Girls Tortured in Britain' is enough for me...[I] don't need to hear about...every single gory detail." Both Joellen and Dave feel that TV programs and advertisements insult their intelligence and waste precious time. They note that, when they briefly rented a condo with a television during their move, squabbles erupted between the two children over the use of the TV and VCR.

Relative newcomers to the no-TV world, the Stellings are learning (as have the other three families) that other people may feel threatened or defensive about their not having television. One family member has refused to visit their home because they do not have TV and one of Dave's former friends ended the friendship saying, "You think you're better than I am because you don't have TV." Both Joellen and Dave now are careful about raising the subject and if someone asks if they saw a particular TV show they often just say, "Gosh, I missed it." The children sometimes ask to watch TV at a neighbor's house, but have not asked to have television at home. They tell visitors, "We don't have a TV, but we've got a fireplace."

In a way, all of these families are modern-day pioneers. They have sought out a way of life that is quite unusual, even though they are nestled in among the rest of the vast, television-owning world. Further, they have done this persistently, over many years, in the face of the disapprobation of at least some friends and family members. The parents all remain highly satisfied with their status as non-owners of television. If anything, they appear to have less inclination to acquire a TV as time goes on. Indeed, it is hard to believe that acquiring a TV would not have an impact on the tempo or substance of these families' active lives.

We are, of course, dealing with a "snapshot" of each family here, not with an ongoing film or video tape. It is possible that any or all of the families could change their minds and become television owners tomorrow. It is significant to note, though, that they have all persevered for at least 5 years (and for an average of almost 13 years) in their original decision.

Inner Resources

A common belief held by the no-TV parents is that it is very important for their children to develop *inner resources*—to think and act for themselves in a moral and responsible manner. They characterize such children as "self-sufficient," "resourceful," and capable of finding "things to do on their own." This quality is something the no-TV parents strive to foster in many ways, just one of which is not having television in the home. It may be, however, that not having television is a uniquely effective way to help children develop their inner resources. We will examine this issue more fully in Chapter 8, after we have reviewed literature that addresses the impact of television on children and families.

Preview

In the chapters that follow we will explore the scientific literature that pertains to various thoughts, justifications, and speculations the no-TV parents raise regarding television generally and its effects on children in particular. In some instances we will examine journalistic sources of information as well. We have not attempted to write a textbook on television's documented effects; such texts already exist (e.g., Comstock, 1991; Condry, 1989; Liebert & Sprafkin, 1988; Singer & Singer, 2001; Strasberger & Wilson, 2002). Rather, we have endeavored to shine some scientific light on specific intuitions expressed by the no-TV pioneers—a group of people who truly view television from a unique perspective within contemporary North American culture.

Chapter 2 addresses the issue of the time taken up by television in TV homes and how that time use may impact other activities. Research findings regarding program content—in particular, aggression and sex—are discussed in Chapter 3. Chapter 4 asks whether people can become addicted to television and examines how such a process might come about. Television's impact on cognition, or thinking, is considered in Chapter 5. In Chapter 6 we look at how television influences the development of reading skills in children. The nature of the television business and the central role of advertising in commercial television is the focus of Chapter 7. Chapter 8 defines inner resources, summarizes the earlier chapters, and relates the information therein to the development of inner resources in children. The last chapter asks the question, "Is living without television for you?"

Chapter 2

Time and Television

Even if you don't look at the potential negative things that come with the set, just the time...it steals from you.... If you're sitting around watching, you're not getting...things ...done.

– Nelson Field

We do a lot of crafts and we just always have so much to do. If we had a television, I don't know when we could have time to watch it.... [We'd] have to let something else go, that we feel is important.... We don't have time for all the things we want to do now.

– Barbara Field

Looking at my children's daily lives (and at my own and Eve's life) it is clear that none of us have any *time* for television. If we had television, we would have to make time for it; in other words, sacrifice something else of value.

– Adam Lake

When my husband and I were first living together, at the beginning of his medical residency, we were afraid that the time constraints would leave us no time for each other. We decided to remove one distraction by not having a TV.

– Laura Lott

I don't remember whose idea it was, but...the basic concept
was the lack of time that we were going to have to interact.
And...still to this day...is a lack of time. ...If I watch the
television for an hour [between] 6 o'clock [and] 9 o'clock,
that's not an hour out of the day, that's a third of the time I
have to be with the family.

– Ben Lott

People say, "Well, what do you *do?*" We have never found
ourselves sitting down for an evening going, "What do we
do? Gosh...I don't know what to do." We've always run out
of time at the end of the day. We always wonder, "Where did
the time go?"

– Joellen Stelling

A college professor of mine—in humanities—referred to
television as "time-wasted drivel." That was 1977. It has not
improved.

– Dave Stelling

All of our no-TV parents indicated in one way or another that
they thought watching television would not be a good use of their time or
their children's time. And, as a strategy for maximizing time use, getting
rid of the TV does not seem like an all together unreasonable thing to do.
But it is interesting to consider what scientific investigations have
uncovered regarding people's use of time in relation to television.

When social scientists first began to explore the impact of
television in the 1950s and 1960s, one of the first issues to be addressed
was the matter of time use. Did television lead people to reorder their
priorities and forsake important things in life in order to be entertained by
TV? It almost seems that it would be simple to measure time spent
viewing and time spent doing other things and make the appropriate
comparisons. But, in reality, measuring time use has been a complicated
undertaking.

Measures of TV-Viewing Time

Probably the best known and most frequently used measure of
television watching is the simple appraisal of whether the TV set is on or
not. This is one of the main measures used by Nielsen Media Research
in arriving at the ratings for the various TV shows that most people see

daily. Because of the simplicity of this measure and also because it has now been in use for many years, it can be used to summarize trends in television use over the years. Nielsen data for the years from 1970 to 2000 show a gradual upward trend in the amount of time U.S. television-owning families have their TVs on per day. This can be seen in Table 1. The average for recent years has been over 7 hours per day—a significant time investment by almost anybody's reckoning.

The Nielsen organization also uses a device called the "people meter," which collects (via a hand-held key pad) information on who is in the room while the TV is on. People meter data, which have been available since 1988, show men in 2000 watching an average of 4 hours and 11 minutes per day, women an average of 4 hours and 46 minutes per day, teenagers 3 hours and 4 minutes per day, and younger children 3 hours and 7 minutes daily (Television Bureau of Advertising, 2002). Again, the figures represent significant time expenditures that lend credibility to the no-TV parents' concerns about time.

TV afficionados will be aware, however, that sometimes a set is on in the room but the occupants of the room pay little or no attention to it. Because of this, some researchers have asked people to estimate their viewing time retrospectively—for the previous day, say, or week. Others have asked people to keep an on-going time diary, noting their activities (including television watching) for a day or for several days. Measurement techniques such as viewing estimates, time diaries, and people meters are, of course, subject to the frailties of human memory, attention, and/or dexterity. As such they are, like the global measure of the TV's being on, imperfect (Huston & Wright, 1998). However, most measures do correlate positively with one another, so even though we do not have a perfect measure, we can feel some sense of confidence because we know the findings tend to veer in similar directions no matter what measure is used.

A very few investigators have actually gone to the heroic length of putting video cameras in people's homes to watch *them* watch TV. One such study found that, among other things, people sometimes engaged in the following activities while viewing: reading, sorting laundry, preparing meals, ironing, exercising, singing, wrestling, disciplining children, eating, sleeping, playing cards, and talking on the phone (Bechtel, Achelpohl, & Akers, 1972). More recently, other researchers did time-lapse video-recordings of the rooms in which families watched television. For 10 days 460 individuals in 99 families were recorded every 1.2 seconds, when they were in a room with a TV

Table 1
*Average daily viewing time, by year, for U.S. television households, 1970
- 2000.* (Data presented with permission of the Television Bureau of
Advertising, 2002; source: Nielsen Media Research).

Year	Time TV is "On" in average TV home, per day	Year	Time TV is "On" in average TV home, per day
1970	5 hours, 56 minutes	1987	7 hours, 1 minute
1971	6 hours, 2 minutes	1988	7 hours, 3 minutes
1972	6 hours, 12 minutes	1989	7 hours, 1 minute
1973	6 hours, 15 minutes	1990	6 hours, 53 minutes
1974	6 hours, 14 minutes	1991	7 hours, 0 minutes
1975	6 hours, 7 minutes	1992	7 hours, 5 minutes
1976	6 hours, 18 minutes	1993	7 hours, 13 minutes
1977	6 hours, 10 minutes	1994	7 hours, 16 minutes
1978	6 hours, 17 minutes	1995	7 hours, 17 minutes
1979	6 hours, 28 minutes	1996	7 hours, 11 minutes
1980	6 hours, 36 minutes	1997	7 hours, 12 minutes
1981	6 hours, 45 minutes	1998	7 hours, 15 minutes
1982	6 hours, 48 minutes	1999	7 hours, 26 minutes
1983	7 hours, 2 minutes	2000	7 hours, 35 minutes
1984	7 hours, 8 minutes		
1985	7 hours, 10 minutes		
1986	7 hours, 8 minutes		

that was turned on (Anderson, Lorch, Field, Collins, & Nathan, 1986). The investigators found that TV sets played to empty rooms 14.7% of the time. Further, when people were present, their attention to television was influenced by how old they were. There was a pronounced rise in visual attention to the TV set between the ages of 1 and 5 years. The 5-year-olds paid attention to an operating television over 70% of the time that they were in the room with it. Attention to TV dropped slightly and leveled off at about 70% for the remainder of the childhood years. Adults' attention to TV dropped off further, to just under 60%. Findings such as these suggest that it often may be more accurate to say people "monitor" television than to say they "view" it (see Comstock, 1991).

So there are many facts and human tendencies that must be taken into account when one attempts to assess the amount of time television absorbs in a typical family. It is clear that people do not always just sit and stare at the set. But in most North American homes the television is a constant presence—either as a backdrop to other activities or as a central focus—a great many hours every week. Researchers who have devoted a good deal of their lives to studying television's role in people's lives suggest that 2 to 3 hours per person per day of viewing television is a conservative estimate (Huston et al., 1992; Kubey & Csikszentmihalyi, 1990).

Consider the ramifications of that. Robert Kubey and Mihalyi Csikszentmihalyi (1990) have analyzed time expenditures for a typical U.S. lifetime. If you live to be 70 years old, they argue, and sleep an average of 8 hours a night (1/3 of a day), you will have 47 *waking years* (2/3 of your 70 years) in which to live your life. As Americans typically have about 5½ hours of free time per day (23% of a day), you can expect about 16 *waking years* (23% of your 70 years) of free time. If one views television an average of the conservative estimate of 2½ hours a day (10.4% of a day), he or she will spend over 7 *waking years* (10.4% of 70 years) watching TV during his or her lifetime. That means that one will be spending about 44% (7/16) of one's lifetime leisure watching television.

Bear in mind that we are estimating *averages* here. There are large individual differences across people as to how much television they view or monitor. For example, one study of New York City homemakers found that 10% of the sample watched TV for more than 55 hours in the week they were studied (about 8 hours per day or more); only 1% watched no TV at all. Average viewing time was 29 hours (Barwise & Ehrenberg, 1988).

In the previous chapter we established that 99% of U.S. households with children have television. Now we know that a television is turned on in those homes an average of over 7 hours a day and that children and teenagers are in the room with the operating TV over 3 hours a day on average, 2½ if we accept the conservative estimate. It seems clear that the *potential* for wasting time exists. But we need to know more about two things: 1) What would people be doing if they were not watching TV? and 2) What really happens to a person when he or she is watching? We will address these questions in the next two sections.

What Activities Does Television Displace?

Television underwent explosive growth in the United States very shortly after it was introduced. Only about 10% of U.S. homes had a television set in 1950; by 1960, 90% of homes had TV (Liebert & Sprafkin, 1988). As we have said, the figure now is well over 98%. The pattern of TV's rapid take-over is of importance because it highlights the relatively small window of opportunity researchers have to study TV "haves" and "have nots" when television first permeates an area. Studies that seek to describe the ways in which television changes people's lives in comparison to existence without television really have to be done quickly, near the beginning of TV's introduction, or the no-TV comparison group will all but disappear. All this is to say that not many studies looked at changes in TV owners' lives during the early years of television. Nevertheless, some did (e.g., Himmelweit, Oppenheim, & Vince, 1958; Robinson, 1972, 1977; Schramm, Lyle, & Parker, 1961; Williams, 1986).

It is interesting that these studies, which were done in the U.S., Britain, and several other countries around the globe, very often revealed startlingly similar results. Generally, during the first flush of television, people in TV households reallocated their time. Most notably, they went to fewer movies, listened to the radio less, did less reading (of magazines, comics, and books), and slept less. To a somewhat lesser extent they decreased time spent on housework, hobbies, socializing outside the home, and church attendance (see Comstock, 1991).

So it would seem that the answer to the question "What does television displace?" is simple. It displaces the things we have just listed —movies, radio, reading, sleeping, etc. To some extent, of course, this is true. But it is interesting to consider some of the ways in which various investigators have interpreted these facts about displacement (see Mutz, Roberts, & van Vuuren, 1993). First, it has been suggested that television simply displaces activities that *serve similar functions*—other media-related activities (Himmelweit et al., 1958). So a half-hour of reading for entertainment may turn into a half-hour of watching TV. Second, it may be the case that TV displaces "marginal" or unstructured activities that have little importance in people's lives—things like hanging out or daydreaming (Himmelweit et al., 1958). In this view, TV is a *default activity* that we engage in when we do not have anything better to do. We are not giving up much of anything to watch it. Third, it may be that when a new medium comes along and "takes over" the way television did, preexisting media are pressured to redefine themselves. The entire media landscape becomes *functionally reorganized* (Brown, Cramond, & Wilde, 1974). Back in the earliest days of television, for example, there were a lot of dramatic shows and comedy shows on radio. When television so effectively took over these functions, radio became mainly a music and news medium. So nobody can listen to soap operas on radio any more because the medium of radio has been reorganized. This, too, surely plays into the ways TV owners (as well as non-owners) use other media.

It is quite possible, of course, that all of these interpretations of the time allocation data are partially correct. But in our view there are important considerations to raise regarding all three.

First, regarding the "similar functions" explanation, we believe one has to be aware of the special importance of reading (see Comstock, 1991). While printed material and television *are* both mass media, the skills required to decode and digest a book—even a comic book—are far more advanced and difficult to acquire than those necessary for enjoying television. We are going to return to the topic of reading in Chapter 6 but, for now, perhaps we can agree that it is something most parents wish their children to do well and that takes a significant time investment for most children to learn. Placing TV, books, magazines, and comics all under the label "mass media" does not make them equivalent. In fact, it glosses over an important difference in how people spend time with and without TV.

Second, regarding the "marginal or default activity" interpretation, we may legitimately question whether so-called "marginal" activities are really unimportant. Who gets to decide that hanging out or daydreaming is "marginal?" That certainly would not be the opinion of Isaac Greenwald—our no-TV 13-year-old whose favorite leisure activity is daydreaming. Comstock (1991) has argued that if TV adds an hour per day of media use to people's schedules, then getting rid of the TV would lead to spending that hour some other way—more likely on something "familiar and convenient" (p. 79) than on something novel. But our no-TV families suggest that a "familiar and convenient" activity may often be conversation with family members or simple contemplation. And these are vastly different from television-watching in a number of ways. We believe that they may oil the practical and emotional gears of the family, teach children language and other social skills, enable displays of respect and affection, encourage confrontation of psychological problems, and/or serve as a basis for creative accomplishments (see, for example, Dunn, 1996; Hughes, 1998; Siegal, 1996; Sutton-Smith, 1997). They are, perhaps, not unimportant at all.

Third, we would like to expand the "functional reorganization" notion. In addition to the new medium's reorganizing preexisting media, we believe a case can be made that it reorganizes families as well. Consider a 13-year-old who, unlike Isaac Greenwald, has grown up in a home with TV. Perhaps the TV has been a default activity in this family for years. Rather than talking about emotional upsets or daydreaming about the future, this child has, with the tacit encouragement of his parents, turned to television. Little problems may have long gone unaddressed. Perhaps they have even grown larger as a result of being ignored. If this family tries to remove television now, after years of relying on it, it is possible it will upset the equilibrium of the family. The family may have organized itself around the TV. We offer this scenario only as a hypothesis regarding what could happen in some families. The preexisting nature of a particular family would almost certainly play a role in its reaction to losing television.

So television does appear to have a consistent effect on certain behaviors. People generally read, sleep, listen to the radio, and visit friends less often when they have TV than when they do not. How we interpret these behavior changes is still a matter for debate. There are those who see them as rather insignificant. Indeed, it is tempting to interpret them this way, if only to convince ourselves that television is not a damaging force in our individual and collective lives. But the case can also be made that the trade-offs engendered by television are undesirable, that they work against children's development and healthy relationships within families. Our no-TV families would no doubt argue for the latter interpretation.

Experiences While Watching Television

Another type of data relevant to the time people expend on television has been generated by the *experience sampling method*, or

ESM. This method attempts to get a detailed account of people's use of time in their natural environments, but it does so without relying on memory, cumbersome time diaries, or the prying eye of a camera. The ESM was used by Kubey and Csikszentmihalyi (1990) in a study of TV viewing and everyday experience. It involves paging or "beeping" study participants randomly throughout the day. Participants agree to fill out activity information forms each time they are beeped. The forms, which take about 2 minutes to complete, ask questions about where participants are, what they are doing, who they are with, and what they are thinking and feeling. More versatile than a camera placed in a participant's living room, the experience sampling method provides numerous, immediate glimpses of participants' lives no matter what room they are in and whether they are home or not. Further, it solicits reports on thoughts and feelings—experiences outside the view of any camera.

One hundred seven Chicago-area working adults participated in this study. They ranged in age from 18 to 63 years and were White, Black, and Hispanic. Participants were beeped 7 to 9 times daily for a period of 1 week. All beeps occurred between the hours of 8 AM and 10 PM. So the investigators collected a *sample* of the participants' daily experiences of (hence the label "experience sampling method"). Based on the sample, Kubey and Csikszentmihalyi were able to make some interesting general statements about the prominence of television in adults' lives, about what they do and how they feel when they are watching, and about differences between light and heavy TV viewers.

When participants were paged, TV-watching was the main activity in which they were engaged for 7.2% of all beeps over the week of the study. It was a secondary activity another 2.8% of the time. In total, then, respondents were exposed to TV during 10% of the times they were signaled. Kubey and Csikszentmihalyi estimate that participants watched TV about 1.4 hours each day, between 8 AM and 10 PM. (They may, of course, have continued to watch after 10 PM, but they would not have been beeped during later hours.) Watching television was by far the most time-consuming of any activity done at home for the adults in this study. They spent a total of 25% of their time at home watching TV. When the investigators looked at how respondents used their leisure hours (a shorter period of time than "time at home"), they found television took up an even greater percentage—about 40% of all leisure time. Over 90% of all television viewing took place at home. People watched with other family members about twice as often as they watched by themselves.

But what were participants doing and feeling while watching

TV? Their reports revealed that 63.5% of the time they were doing something else while watching TV. Most often the accompanying activity was eating or talking. At other times people smoked, did chores, read, took care of their children, or engaged in grooming activities while watching. This time sharing of television and other activities was the rule for the participants in this study. Very few consistently watched TV without doing something else at the same time. Kubey and Csikszentmihalyi note that people who have had years of experience with television, as most of us in the U.S. have, may view less intently than newcomers to the medium. This assertion is in keeping with the observation of one of our no-TV parents, Eve Greenwald, that families with TV talk frequently during programs.

If television were mainly just a benign, ignored background to the real stuff of life, we could argue that there is little cause to worry about it. However, ESM data revealed that when television accompanied other activities, people tended to concentrate somewhat less on those activities and to feel somewhat more passive than when television was not part of the background (Kubey & Csikszentmihalyi, 1990). So even when it is not being attended to, it appears to exert a subtle influence on subjective perceptions of activity/passivity and concentration.

Recall that when ESM participants filled out activity information forms they noted their moods. They also noted how alert, strong, and active they felt. If beeped while watching television, they frequently gave themselves low mood ratings—with low levels of cheerfulness, friendliness, happiness, and sociability. (This was particularly true of heavy viewers.) Viewers in general also reported low levels of activity, strength, alertness, and excitement during viewing. In fact, the only activity that rated lower than TV-watching on these measures was resting. Even a behavior category called "idling," which included waiting, not doing anything, and daydreaming was accompanied by a more positive mood and more activation than watching TV. Despite low ratings on mood and activation, television-watching was a popular activity and one that people frequently said they wished they were doing at any given moment. Perhaps, as Kubey and Csikszentmihalyi suggest, its appeal is exactly *that* it is a very relaxing and undemanding activity that engenders passivity in viewers.

Kubey and Csikszentmihalyi ranked all the participants in their study according to the total amount of television they watched. They designated the top third of the group as "heavy viewers" and the bottom third as "light viewers." This enabled them to make some interesting comparisons. Light viewers talked twice as much as heavy viewers when they were at home. Light viewers spent less time at home than heavy viewers and more time walking or standing. In general, during *all* activities heavy viewers reported less concentration, less sense of control, less positive moods, and less of a sense of relaxation than light viewers. These findings caused the investigators to speculate about why some people become such heavy users of television. They acknowledged that a lot of factors may play into the decision to view or not to view. But they felt that it may generally be the case that heavy viewers are more uncomfortable and anxious than light viewers—especially when they are alone and have nothing to do—and turn to television as a means of creating a sense of order and blunting a sad mood. So it is possible that some of us become heavy viewers because of psychological discomfort. It is also possible that heavy television use actually stimulates psychological discomfort. As Kubey and Csikszentmihalyi put it, "We cannot rule out that spending tens of thousands of hours watching television might not reduce a person's ability to give shape to free time. ...It seems likely that heavy viewing helps perpetuate itself" (1990, p. 165).

Kubey and Csikszentmihalyi's innovative study provides a unique and intimate view of people's use of television. It reaffirms that seemingly average people spend a lot of time with television and often do other activities while watching. It dramatically demonstrates how very passive and relaxed people tend to be when they are viewing. It shows that there are psychological differences between heavy and light users of television and raises the possibility that heavy use is partly responsible for anxiety and psychological discomfort during times when one has nothing to do.

Are these findings and the others noted above cause for alarm? That, of course, is for each individual and each family to decide. Our no-TV families have decided in one way, but there are many more families whose opinions differ markedly from theirs. Consider the use of time in the lives of the two families described below.

Two Different Families; Two Different Lives

Our no-TV parents have chosen a way of life that is extreme in that it involves no television use in the home. The other extreme, which probably occurs with a good deal more frequency, would be a family that keeps the TV running during all its waking hours. As it happens, a description of just such a family appeared a few years ago in *The*

Washington Post Magazine (Finkel, 1994). It is interesting to contrast a day in the life of this family with a day in the life of one of our no-TV families. To keep it simple, we will focus on the mothers' activities during one day.

Bonnie, the 35-year-old mother of the heavy-viewing family, has a bachelor's degree. She is a full-time homemaker with two children, 6 and 7, and a husband who works as a financial officer. She is an unabashed appreciator of television and estimates she watches about 63 hours a week. Her husband is supportive of her fascination with the medium.

During one of the days that she was followed by the reporter, Bonnie got up at 8:20 AM and immediately switched on the TV in her bedroom. She watched parts of *CBS This Morning* and *Today* before she went down to the kitchen. There, she turned to *Regis and Kathie Lee* while her children sat at the table watching a cartoon on another TV set. During the day, when the children were at school, Bonnie watched parts of four talk shows, some soap operas, and some "infotainment" offerings. *Maury Povich* was on when she left to pick up the children at school. It was still on when the three returned, just in time to hear about a 600-pound woman who was in a weight-loss program that allowed conjugal visits. The woman's husband related how much he *really* liked his wife's body. (An announcement noted that, should Bonnie tune in again the next day, she would see a man who has had his private parts enlarged.) Next, she watched *Sally Jessy Raphael*, who was interviewing mothers and daughters who shared the same boyfriend. After watching sitcoms and local news while fixing dinner, the whole family ate while watching the national news. After *Jeopardy*, Bonnie watched a line-up of six sitcoms and then tuned in the *Tonight* show. Her husband and children joined her for some of the evening. They had certain family favorites they usually watched together, including *Home Improvement*, *Seinfeld*, and *Married...With Children*. Bonnie routinely fell asleep with *David Letterman* playing on the bedroom TV.

While the TV was on, Bonnie typically did household chores, read the newspaper, and worked on crafts. She even read books (she was currently reading one by Howard Stern) and read with her daughter (who was reading a book about a sitcom character). She felt strongly that her children were sweet, well-behaved, and trustworthy. Her husband made the argument that TV only displaces marginal activities and, like Bonnie, he did not worry about its effects on his family.

Compare Bonnie's daily experiences with television to a day in the life of Eve Greenwald. We have selected Eve here because, like Bonnie, she is a full-time homemaker and has two children who are in school. We selected a weekday from Eve's activity log at random. Eve was up before 6:30, having breakfast and getting her daughter ready for school. After Anna left, Eve did house chores by herself for about an hour, read for half an hour, and then worked in her garden for most of the morning. At lunch time she drove her son to someone's house and then settled down by herself to look over some new songs that she might begin rehearsing. She learned the end of a song she had been working on and then listened to music while she did some transcribing and had a bite to eat. At 3 o'clock her daughter came home from school. She chatted with her husband and daughter for about half an hour and then took her daughter and a friend to see a neighbor's new goat. She visited with the friend's mother for awhile and then went to the grocery store, library, and post office. She visited with another friend in a store. When she got home she cleaned her kitchen and chatted again with her husband. She played the piano with her daughter for half an hour and then the family sat down together for dinner. After that, she cleaned up, checked on her garden, and spent the rest of the evening talking with the family and working on her activity log. She went to bed at about 9:30.

Concluding Thoughts

In this chapter we have learned that people have a great fondness—some might call it a weakness—for TV. They use it a lot, more as the years go by, and some, like Bonnie and her family, carry it to an extreme. But there is much more to know about television than just the amount of time it takes up and the activities it displaces. In the next chapter we will examine the content of television programs and explore the research on content effects.

Chapter 3

The Content of Television

[Christina] asked me in the car on the way back from the library, "What does *develop* mean?" Must have heard it on the radio.... And that was one of the things that really scared us about TV.... We were just shocked at what [the children] absorb.... And we thought, "If they're doing that with stuff we want them to hear, what are they doing with stuff [we] don't want them to hear?"

– Dave Stelling

[TV] models a culture that we don't like, that's very violent and it's very overly sexualized.... We struggle around here mightily to remind them that...over the long run, [that] is not healthy, is not really good.

– Ben Lott

When we're in a motel and have the television on some of the things that they flash on the screen are just shocking, you know.

– Barbara Field

[TV] was...putting very frightening ideas in my head that I had never thought of.

– Joellen Stelling

Some of our kids...are at risk for a lot of adolescent behaviors. And I think that all that's just stimulated and reinforced on television, a lot.

– Laura Lott

When I'm making rounds at the hospital and looking at the
TVs in everybody's room...you catch...what was the
one?...mothers who sleep with their sons, or something, you
know.... It's just these crazy things.... What happens...,by
doing that, is you promote that as sort of a normal life.... Like
all these gangster things.... That's just sort of gotten to
where, you know, that's sort of "normal."
                                                     – Ben Lott

[TV] desensitizes people to [the] feelings of others' being
injured. They see it all the time, on the television.
                                                  – Nelson Field

Both kids...they're just starting to understand what's real and
what's not real.... Carlton was at a ball game this summer and
got to run the bases with [the mascot]. And Carlton came
back to the seat and Christina said, "Carlton, is he real?! Is
he real?!"... They don't understand it's not a dog. So that,
too, reinforces our not wanting them to watch TV.
                                               – Joellen Stelling

I love beauty and kindness. Neither are often represented on
TV and never as well as in nature, art, books,...[or] in daily
practice.
                                               – Eve Greenwald

No aspect of television has been so hotly debated and frequently
criticized as the actual behaviors it depicts and the things that are said by
its various hosts, guests, commentators, spokespersons, and characters.
This is what the title of the present chapter refers to—the *content* of
television. In the United States there has long been concern about the
levels of violence in television programming and, in recent years, critics
have become increasingly alarmed by the casual depiction of sexual
intentions and behaviors.

In light of general uneasiness over these particular content issues
it is interesting that, for our no-TV parents, issues of violence and sex in
and of themselves were not noticeably more important than any of the
many other issues that troubled them about television. To be sure, they
spoke generally about the shocking nature of contemporary programming,
but this was clearly just one of many concerns that confirmed their
decision not to own a TV. Perhaps the violent or sexual content of

television was not uppermost in their minds because it had been years since any of them had been regularly exposed to it.

But the vast majority of us *have* been exposed to quite a bit of it. We turn now to a description of some of the massive scientific literature that has addressed televised violence and its effects on humans, particularly children.

Prevalence of Violence on Television

Violence is a staple ingredient of television programming, in shows aimed at adults as well as those designed for child audiences. For many years George Gerbner, former Dean of the Annenberg School of Communications, and his colleagues have been monitoring levels of violence in televised entertainment programming. Their long-running investigation shows trends in violent programming over a period that extends from the 1960s up to the 1990s. *Violence*, in Gerbner's assessments, includes the use of physical force that threatens, injures, or kills human or human-like characters. Both intentional and unintentional acts are included, as are both humorous and serious forms of attack (G. Gerbner, personal communication, October 16, 1986).

Sticking with this rather broad definition of violence over the many years of monitoring television content, Gerbner and colleagues have found high and quite stable levels of violence in both prime-time network programs and in children's programs that are broadcast on Saturday mornings (see Huston & Wright, 1998; Liebert & Sprafkin, 1988). During the years from 1973 to 1993, for example, 71.2% of prime-time shows contained violence, as did 92% of children's programs. There were 5.3 violent episodes per hour, on average, in prime time and a whopping 23 such episodes per hour in the children's programs (Gerbner, Morgan, & Signorielli, 1993, cited in Huston & Wright, 1998). Every year since 1967 when the study began, children's programs have been more violent than the prime-time shows (see Liebert & Sprafkin, 1988; Huston & Wright, 1998).

In recent years, two new studies that monitor television violence have added to our knowledge about the content of television. One of these studies was carried out in three yearly installments by the UCLA Center for Communication Policy (Cole, 1997). This investigation was funded by the broadcast television networks under pressure from former Senator Paul Simon (D-Ill.) and the U.S. Senate. The other study, conducted in response to the same pressures, was carried out by researchers at a number of different locations around the country and was funded by the cable networks (*National Television Violence Study*, 1997, 1998). Both studies were funded but not initiated by the television industry. Investigators were guaranteed independence in constructing a methodology, collecting data, and reporting findings.

Both investigations defined violence in much the same way that Gerbner did. However, they examined a greater sampling of programs and a more diverse set of program types. Further, they scrutinized how the violence was presented and attempted to differentiate programs according to whether they would be likely to have adverse effects on viewers. For our purposes, let's just look at their general conclusions.

The UCLA study (Cole, 1997) monitored prime-time series, specials, movies, Saturday morning children's programs, and on-air promotions to see whether they raised concerns about the violence they aired. Over the 3 years of the study, it found lessening cause for concern. It is important to realize that this does not mean there was less violence, but simply that the violent episodes more often met the researchers' standards for showing violence responsibly. The standards for responsible violence included provisos such as the following: violence should be realistically depicted; perpetrators should often show remorse; and violence should sometimes take place off-camera (Cole, 1997).

The *National Television Violence Study* (1997) monitored cable programs for the most part. An investigation of series, movies, specials, and children's shows led researchers to conclude that TV violence was not usually very graphic; however, its negative consequences (e.g., pain and suffering) were rarely shown, it usually did not result in punishment of aggressors, it was rarely embedded in a program with an antiviolent theme, and it did pose risks for viewers. As to the "reality" shows—which include tabloid news, talk shows, police shows, and documentaries—38% of them included some visible violence and another 18% included talk that revolved around violence. Thus, a total of 56% of such programs included some level of violent content.

So violence continues to be very prevalent on television. This is especially true of children's programs. There are some indications that the violence has been presented in a more responsible fashion by the broadcast networks in recent years, but this has not altered the fact that there is still a tremendous amount of it on TV daily. The no-TV parents' concerns about violent content appear to be well-founded.

But does televised violence really have any impact on viewers? In our experience, most people express the belief that it does not influence *them*. (See also Bushman & Huesmann, 2001.) However, we should examine some of the scientific findings before concluding that TV violence is not a legitimate social problem.

Televised Violence and Aggressive Behavior

Researchers' interest in whether and how televised violence might affect people's actual behavior dates from the well-known Bobo doll studies of Albert Bandura and colleagues (Bandura, 1965; Bandura, Ross, & Ross, 1961, 1963). In these studies, young children watched a film of an adult aggressing in various distinct ways against an inflated plastic Bobo doll. (Bobo invited hitting, as he popped back up after he was knocked down.) Investigators found that children did indeed imitate aggressive behaviors they saw on film and that, even if they did not engage in these actions spontaneously, they were *able* to imitate them if offered a small incentive to do so (Bandura, 1965).

These findings had troubling implications regarding the aggression routinely depicted on television. But they did involve a fairly artificial or unusual situation, in that the children were shown the film by a stranger who later led them into a playroom that contained the exact Bobo doll they had seen on film. And hitting a Bobo doll is, after all, just a form of play—not the kind of aggression that would cause most parents to worry. The possibility existed that under conditions more typical of children's real lives the imitation of aggression would not have occurred.

These considerations heralded a large, new wave of research that approached the study of video violence and viewers' aggressive behavior from many different angles. Some of the new studies inquired whether children would choose to play more with toys that had an aggressive theme after viewing a violent cartoon than after seeing a nonviolent program (e.g., Lovaas, 1961). Other studies looked at children's interpersonal aggression—pushing, hitting, or wrestling behaviors with other youngsters—following exposure to aggressive or nonaggressive TV programs (e.g., Steuer, Applefield, & Smith, 1971). Still others measured children's television-watching habits and correlated them with their classmates' reports of how aggressive they were at school (e.g., Lefkowitz, Eron, Walder, & Huesmann, 1972). Other investigators correlated adolescents' preferences for violent TV with their levels of deviant behaviors—such as being defiant and aggressive (McIntyre & Teevan, 1972). One study followed a group of children from age 8 all the way to age 30 and correlated their exposure to violent TV at age 8 with their criminal records at 30 years of age (Huesmann, 1986; Huesmann, Eron, Lefkowitz, & Walder, 1984). In a few cases, large groups of people for whom television had just become available were studied as to their aggressive behaviors pre- and post-television (e.g., Williams, 1986). Eventually, after literally hundreds of studies had been done, some industrious investigators collected and statistically analyzed the findings of whole groups of studies, using meta-analyses (e.g., Hearold, 1986; Paik & Comstock, 1994; Wood, Wong, & Chachere, 1991).

What is striking about all these different approaches is that the vast majority of findings support the existence of a link between televised aggression and people's aggressive behavior. All of the studies mentioned in the paragraph above found a statistically significant link between the two. So the findings have held up using different ways of determining exposure to media violence, different ways of measuring aggressive behavior, and using participants of different ages and backgrounds. In fact, researchers who recently reviewed 40 years of research on this issue noted:

> Over the past few decades many governmental and professional organizations have conducted exhaustive reviews of the scientific literature on the relationship between media violence and aggressive behavior. These investigations have consistently documented how media violence, across various genres, is related to the aggressive behavior of many children, adolescents, and adults (*National Television Violence Study*, 1997, p. 9).

The sheer weight of the evidence may give one pause even if one does not think himself or herself personally affected by television's predilection for violent programming.

An issue tied to that of aggressive behavior is raised by the parents of Christina and Carlton Stelling who, at 3 and 4, are not yet fully able to grasp the distinction between fantasy and reality. If televised violence is seen as "real," might it have a different effect on people than if it is seen as fantasy? A study done with 10- to 13-year-old children indicates that TV violence appearing to be real stimulates more aggression in viewers than fantasy violence (Atkin, 1983). In this study a fight scene was presented either as a news clip or as an ad for a movie. Children who had seen either version reacted more aggressively than children who had seen no aggression at all. But the youngsters who saw the scene as "news" were even more aggressive than those who were told it was a movie ad. Similar results have been found with adult participants (Berkowitz & Alioto, 1973; Jo & Berkowitz, 1994). So perhaps Joellen and Dave Stelling have a legitimate concern, in light of the fact that their two youngsters would likely see much of what is on TV as, in some sense, real.

It is possible, of course, that the fantasy/reality issue becomes inconsequential as children get older and are able to understand that a great many of the aggressive behaviors they see on TV are fictional. But keep in mind that both children and adults *do* react to fantasy violence. And there is the additional complicating possibility that years of exposure to aggressive acts on television may *desensitize* people to real violence when it happens in the world around them.

Televised Violence and Desensitization to Real Violence

How might an investigator determine whether someone has become desensitized to real-life violence as a result of exposure to TV violence? One possibility would be to create an apparently "real" violent episode and assess participants' reactions to it.

Such an approach was used effectively in the 1970s by two investigators who developed an elaborate means of exposing older children (fifth graders) to aggression that was not real but seemed as if it were (Drabman & Thomas, 1976). The fifth graders watched either an aggressive film or a sports film and then waited, individually, in a room that contained a television monitor. On the monitor they could see two younger children (preschoolers) playing. The older children—the participants in the study—were essentially told that they were babysitting for the younger children, who were in another room. If the younger ones got into trouble, the older child was to leave the room and get an adult's help. The preschool children were actually on videotape and had been directed to pick a fight. The fight progressed to pushing, chasing, and finally to knocking over the video camera, whereupon the monitor in the older child's room went black. The participants were timed as to how long after the beginning of the fight they left the room to seek adult help. Participants who had seen the aggressive film took significantly longer than those who saw the sports film to react to the younger children's fight.

This result has been widely interpreted as evidence that viewing video portrayals of violence really does blunt children's responses to real-life aggression. Because it has been so often cited as evidence, two other investigators recently updated and repeated Drabman and Thomas's experiment to see if its results would hold up for contemporary youngsters (Molitor & Hirsch, 1994). They showed fourth and fifth graders either a condensed version of *The Karate Kid* (this was the aggressive video) or scenes from summer Olympic games. Once again, children who had seen the violent show took longer than those who saw the nonviolent show to respond to aggression they believed was real. This result occurred even though some of the children participating in the study had seen *The Karate Kid* previously and all of them had likely had many hours of immersion in fictionalized television by the time they reached the fourth and fifth grades.

Desensitization effects are hard to measure for at least two reasons. First, it is hard to create a believable but staged aggressive episode. Second, if desensitization really does occur, it has probably already happened—to a greater or lesser degree—to the vast majority of TV-watching North Americans. So researchers are searching for a way to demonstrate a phenomenon that may already be fully in effect on a wide-spread basis. It is, of course, harder to demonstrate the existence of the phenomenon the closer it gets to its upper limit or ceiling. At this point we do not know how desensitization operates over the long term. Perhaps it dissipates over time; perhaps it accumulates. We hope that further research will make the time course of the desensitization process clear.

The experimental demonstrations of desensitization just described are consistent with the idea that, at least under some circumstances, children can and do become desensitized to the violence they see on television. The extent to which televised aggression has contributed to current levels of callousness in society is uncertain. For now we can say that there is some scientific support for Nelson Field's belief that TV desensitizes people to the feelings of real-life victims.

Televised Violence and the Belief in a Mean World

George Gerbner and his colleagues have proposed that heavy immersion in the world of television may influence people's general view of the *real* world (Gerbner, Gross, Morgan, & Signorielli, 1994; Signorielli & Morgan, 2001). Their proposal is called the *cultivation hypothesis*. Because so much of television programming depicts violence, the cultivation hypothesis predicts that heavy viewers will see the world as a meaner and more menacing place than it really is or than light viewers believe it to be. In fact, these predictions have been borne out in research.

In one study, over 500 adolescents were asked about their beliefs (Gerbner, Gross, Signorielli, Morgan, & Jackson-Beeck, 1979). For example, they were asked to estimate the percentage of people involved in violence in a given year and were given the option of picking 3% or 10% as their answer. The 3% answer was correct. The 10% answer was derived from what television portrays. Consistently, more heavy viewers than light viewers picked the answer that reflected what is shown on TV. Similar results have been found with a large sample of Australian children and adolescents (Pingree & Hawkins, 1981). So heavy viewers' beliefs about the world do appear to be skewed away from reality toward the meaner world of television.

In another study, an experiment, investigators got college students to agree to a prescribed television regimen for a 6-week period (Bryant, Carveth, & Brown, 1981). One group watched very little TV. Two other groups were assigned to watch heavily—28 hours a week or more. Both heavy-viewing groups watched action-packed programs but one group stuck to programs where the "good guys" came out on top and the other group watched mainly shows in which justice did not prevail. Heavy viewers who saw a lot of injustice during the 6-week period ended up with the most fear that they could become crime victims. The heavy viewers who saw the good guys win had moderately elevated fear of becoming victims. Light viewers scored lowest on this measure. Such findings support Ben Lott's contention that what appears repeatedly on television begins to seem "normal."

Scientific investigations, then, suggest that the violence that is so common on TV does have undesirable effects—on people's behavior, on their sensitivity to any aggression that they may witness directly, and on their view of the world as either benign or menacing. Although these effects are disagreeable to most parents, it is important to keep the findings in perspective. Whatever contribution television makes to such objectionable characteristics and beliefs, it is but one of many contributing causes. Whether a particular family sees it as substantial enough to warrant action is really a matter of personal judgment. For their part, our no-TV parents have decided it is a contributing cause that they want to eliminate from their children's home lives.

Prevalence of Sex on Television

Another content issue that was raised by one of the no-TV parents—and that has been raised by a good many TV parents as well—is how and how often sexual behaviors and intentions are spotlighted in television programming. Although there has been far less research on sexual content than on violence in television programming (see Donnerstein & Smith, 2001), some illuminating studies have been done. Over time, there has been both consistency and change in televised sexual content. For one thing, *talking* about sex has routinely been far more common on TV than actual, visual portrayals of sexual behaviors (Buerkel-Rothfuss, 1993; Greenberg et al., 1993; Kunkel et al., 1999; Sapolsky & Tabarlet, 1991). Despite this apparent concession to the sensitive nature of sexual content, however, the topic of sex has come up on TV shows with increasing frequency over the past 2 or 3 decades (Buerkel-Rothfuss, 1993; Huston & Wright, 1998). Sex between people who are not married to one another characteristically outnumbers sex between married people by a margin of 3 or 4 to 1 (Buerkel-Rothfuss, 1993; Truglio, 1993, cited in Huston & Wright, 1998).

One study compared sexual references in prime-time shows in 1989 to similar references in the shows of 1979 (Sapolsky & Tabarlet, 1991). These researchers defined a sexual incident as any explicit depiction of sex, seductive body display, or overt or veiled reference to sexual behavior or organs. They found that use of sexual language held steady between 1979 and 1989, suggestive body displays declined, and sexual touching increased. Explicit depictions of sexual intercourse were quite rare (but not absent) both years. Most of the sex took place between unmarried characters who showed very little concern with the possible consequences of sexual behavior.

Findings like these have been typical. Greenberg and colleagues (1993) looked specifically at soap operas and prime-time shows most watched by ninth and tenth graders. They found more sexual acts per soap opera hour (3.67) than per prime-time hour (2.95). The soaps portrayed mainly long kisses and intercourse; in prime-time there were more diverse sexual depictions, including prostitution and homosexuality. When characters who were not participants in a sexual episode showed a reaction to it, the reaction tended to be negative. The authors estimated that youngsters who watch 9 hours of prime-time TV per week see 27 sexual acts (or references) per week or 1,400 per year.

You can see, perhaps, why no-TV parents, researchers, and other professionals concerned with the healthy development of children are troubled. Television may be playing an important role in children's sexual development, for at least two reasons: 1) they watch so much of it; and 2) many of them get so little information about sex from other sources (Roberts, 1982). If there is little to counteract them or put them in context, the sexual lessons on television may be taken to heart by a lot of children. But what do we know about the effects of televised sexual subject matter on viewers?

Sex on Television and Its Effects on Viewers

As you might imagine, researchers have been extremely reluctant to ask children, especially younger ones, questions of a sexual nature. The societal taboos against sexualizing the lives of children—although not always evident on television—*are* in effect within the research community. Consequently, we have virtually no direct evidence on how television sex may influence children younger than adolescents. Even with adolescents, investigators have been more likely to assess attitudes than to try to obtain measures of actual behaviors.

One study (Strouse & Buerkel-Rothfuss, 1987) found heavier viewing of soap operas and MTV by college students to be associated with more permissive sexual attitudes and behaviors. However, this study was not designed to show whether permissive attitudes prompted TV choices or vice versa. Its authors feel a circumstantial case can be made for TV's influencing attitudes, but their speculations have yet to be confirmed by hard evidence.

Another group of investigators studied 10- to 15-year-old girls' reactions to sexual content in the media (Brown, White, & Nikopoulou, 1993). They found different children had different reactions. Some were *disinterested*. Others (the majority of their participants) were *intrigued* and used media as a safe source of sexual information from which they could learn without actually getting involved in sex. The authors referred to these girls as "active sexual information seekers" (Brown et al., 1993, p. 193). The *resisters* were already in relationships and had become disillusioned with the media's information. These findings raise the possibility that most girls go through a period of heightened sensitivity to media sex on the way to adult sexuality.

The extent to which television's sometimes bizarre, sexualized world may influence the construction of the individual's adult sexuality is unknown at this point. Clearly it would be valuable to know whether television's view of sex infiltrates youngsters' fantasies, behavior, satisfaction, or safety. But research ethics prevent us from prying into young people's private lives to find out. It is almost too facile and obvious to point out that if there were no television in the home, the major source of this uncertainty would be eliminated.

Concluding Thoughts

The no-TV parents raised questions about the sex and violence shown on TV. When scientific studies have looked at the content of television programs they have confirmed without question that TV programming is routinely peppered with violence and with sexual references. Children and adults who view a great deal of television—and there are legions who do—are likely to encounter substantial aggressive and sexual content. Research has documented that televised violence can and often does influence viewers' behaviors, sensitivities, and beliefs. The extent to which sex on TV has similar effects is likely to remain an open question, owing to the ethical questions raised by researching that sensitive topic. In the meantime, busy parents have to make decisions— right now, today, this minute—regarding their children's television use. The no-television decision is but one of many that could be made. In some ways it may be the simplest.

It is important to realize that the picture could all change tomorrow. Television has been violent since its inception and sexual content has been growing over time. But these trends are not written in stone. They could change. Recently V-chip devices have become available, to help parents screen objectionable content. New cable offerings aimed at children are sure to become available as well. But content, of course, is not the only problematic feature of television. There are additional issues to consider, including the question of television addiction, to which we turn next.

Chapter 4

The Question of Addiction

[My] wife and I are addicted to TV, would watch it all the time.

— Ben Lott

When I watch TV I just glom on to it. And I don't pay attention to anybody. I don't just casually watch it.

— Ben Lott

[TV's] almost like a drug for people that have one.

— Dave Stelling

It's like this addiction, and [TV owners] know everybody else around them has it too.

— Eve Greenwald

[One of the children], just by her behavior and by what we know about her personality...is real high risk for smoking, and probably for drinking. She's just that kind of kid. She's very oral and she's real addicted to sugar. I think watching TV would just reinforce that incredibly.

— Laura Lott

The decision [not to have TV] was made before my children's characteristics could be detected, but they now reinforce the decision. [One of the children] has a very addiction-prone personality.

— Eve Greenwald

> Now if people have a set on, I'm as glued to it as anybody
> else.... I could have a conversation here with you and it
> would be very disrupting to have a TV on, because I think
> somehow TV...makes you draw to it.
>
> – Joellen Stelling

Several of the no-TV parents feel either that they themselves are addicted to television or that people in general often are. Two of the no-TV mothers believe that immersion in the world of TV might intensify addictive tendencies they perceive in one of their own children. In fact, such beliefs about the addictive qualities of television are quite common. Survey data have shown that between 2% and 12.5% of adults think that they personally are addicted to TV and that 65% to 70% think *other* people are addicted (Kubey, 1996).

From time to time, articles in the popular press—books, magazines, newspapers—also contend that television addiction is a problem in need of a solution (e.g., Bernard, 1990; Diamond, 1996; Mander, 1978; Stone, 1986; Wilkins, 1982; Winn, 1985). Such items typically focus on *children's* TV-viewing habits and decry the lost experiences that are the inevitable result of heavy television use. It is safe to predict that when authors use words like "addiction" or "drug" in connection with television they will focus on the harmful effects of the medium on viewers. Most of these authors (Mander is an exception) stop short of recommending that television be eliminated from children's lives. Rather, they typically advocate parental control of TV use, often via a menu of possible family rules and regulations.

Our concern here is what the scientific literature has to say about television addiction. Is there such a thing? If so, what might its signs or symptoms be? In addressing these questions, we will begin by taking a look at *attentional inertia*.

Attentional Inertia

"Bet you can't eat just one," boasted a TV ad a few years back. The implication, of course, was that partaking of *some* induced the appetite for *more*. It is interesting that a somewhat similar phenomenon seems to play at least a small role in people's attention to an operating television set. Attentional inertia was discovered by Daniel Anderson and colleagues as they closely watched children while those children watched television (Anderson, Alwitt, Lorch, & Levin, 1979). Each child's pattern of glances to and away from the TV was noted moment by moment, across time.

It turned out that preschool children shifted their attention to and away from the television set very frequently. Attention was often called back to the TV by particular features of a program, such as movement, women's voices, lively music, or animation. Interestingly, in spite of all the fluctuation in attention, if children started watching and continued doing so for 10 or 15 seconds, they were very likely to keep watching. Likewise, if they looked away for 15 seconds or so, they were likely to keep doing that. In the field of physics "inertia" refers to both the tendency of a moving body to keep moving and of a body at rest to remain at rest; attentional inertia is the tendency of attention to remain in the same state over time.

Before we consider how this might relate to addictive TV watching, let's consider some questions that may have occurred to you and that certainly occurred to Anderson and his fellow researchers. First, it seemed possible that sustained attention might be due simply to continuity in the content of the particular program the study's participants were watching. To test this possibility, the investigators looked at children's attention to TV when the content shifted while they were watching (Anderson & Lorch, 1983). Would children show evidence of attentional inertia across boundaries between two different types of program content? Yes, they did. Quoting Anderson and Lorch, "Attentional inertia serves to 'drive' looks across content boundaries" (1983, p. 24). Content changes *may* induce a shift in attention, but if the viewer has already become wrapped up in watching, he or she will probably continue to watch in spite of a change in content.

Another question that might be raised at this point is whether these results apply just to children. Perhaps adults—or infants, for that matter—would respond differently. When this was investigated, viewers of all ages—1-year-olds through adults—showed evidence of attentional inertia (Anderson & Lorch, 1983).

So TV viewers of any age seem to have difficulty watching just a little bit of television, at least once their gaze has been directed toward the TV for about 15 seconds. Once they start to watch, they tend to keep watching. "Bet you can't look for just 15 seconds" might be a fitting slogan. With snack food, as with television, we *can*, of course, eat "just one" or watch for only 15 seconds. But we tend not to. We tend to keep going.

Anderson and Lorch (1983) speculated that attentional inertia is an involuntary tendency of humans that enables one to keep his or her attention focused on dynamic, changing, not-entirely-predictable stimulation. As such, it helps people learn from and adapt to an ever-changing world. It is not specific just to television, but it comes to bear on TV with special force because of the ever-changing nature of television images.

Attentional inertia may help explain why humans get hooked into the energy of television. Clearly, however, it cannot be a full explanation for what some writers have called television *addiction*. For one thing, we all *do* ultimately stop watching and do something else. Even more to the point, some of us stop watching way before others do. In all likelihood, both light and heavy viewers are drawn initially to an operating television by some feature of program content that is of interest to them and then find it increasingly difficult to break a sustained gaze after it has been maintained for a while.

The concept of attentional inertia may help us understand the beginning of the process by which television works its influence on human attention. But it is a short-term effect having to do with how we get drawn in. Understanding it is a little like understanding why people try alcohol and like it initially. It is an important part of the story, but we also need to know why some of us keep doing it to excess.

Longer-Term Attraction to Television

The notion of addiction to TV has been in the literature virtually since the beginning of scientific investigation of the effects of television. Hilde Himmelweit and her colleagues studied 1,854 British school children, 10 to 11 and 13 to 14 years of age, as television was first being introduced into England (Himmelweit, Oppenheim, & Vince, 1958). Although these authors believed addiction not to be simply a matter of viewing heavily, they had to fall back on "viewing hours" as their way of designating the "addicts" in their sample. Accordingly, they examined the heaviest-viewing third of their participants and compared them to the children who watched TV less frequently.

On weekdays, the addicts watched TV half of the time between the end of school and going to bed. This meant they were watching during more than half of their free time on school days. The heavy viewing children at both age levels came disproportionately from the average and lower-than-average intelligence levels. For the younger children only, addicts came more often from working class than middle class homes.

Of special interest are the researchers' findings regarding the personality characteristics of TV-addicted youngsters. These children tended to be insecure and to feel rejected by other children. Their teachers often described them as shy and submissive and as better followers than leaders. Further, they partook heavily of other media— radio, movies, and comic books—as well as television. In general, heavy viewers, more than lighter viewers, desired to have things done for them rather than doing or exploring on their own. Interestingly, they preferred to watch TV in the dark more than children who viewed less TV. The findings were generally in keeping with the view that the TV addicts are withdrawing from reality.

In this analysis, personality predispositions and viewing behavior interact and, in so doing, accentuate addicted children's retreat from the real world with its many challenges and potentials. As the authors put it, "These characteristics [insecurity, fear, and a need for ready-made entertainment] are more likely to be the cause than the result of heavy viewing, but the intensive viewing which addiction entails can only make matters worse" (Himmelweit et al., 1958, p. 29).

Another group of early investigators studied North American children during the first decade of commercial TV's availability in the U.S. and Canada (Schramm, Lyle, & Parker, 1961). These authors stated that TV addicts do exist and that there are two kinds of them. One type of addict seeks excitement and presumably finds it in many television shows. This type of person feels bored and uncomfortable in the absence of excitement. The other type of addict finds reality of any type unpleasant and uses television as a means of avoiding reality and being soothed by fantasy. Both types of addicts may have been taught they should not watch much TV and, if this is so, they may actually get an additional, perverse kind of pleasure in doing something they know to be wrong. In either case, Schramm and his colleagues felt that TV may exacerbate addictive tendencies but does not cause them to begin with. As they put it, "Some children have in them the seeds of addiction; others do not" (Schramm et al., 1961, p. 168).

Bear in mind that these conceptualizations of television addiction are highly speculative. They are interesting in that they represent early ways of thinking about television use and they both tie TV use to viewers' personality characteristics. But in both the British and North American studies "addiction" essentially meant nothing more than heavy use. As such, it lacked the special, "iron-grip," potentially life-diminishing quality that we associate with addictions to alcohol or drugs.

Before moving on to further consideration of addiction, let's remind ourselves of some pertinent findings that were covered in Chapter 2 of this book. Recall that Kubey and Csikszentmihalyi (1990), using the Experience Sampling Method (ESM), found the adults in their study spent 40% of all their leisure time between 8:00 AM and 10:00 PM in the presence of television. Recall, too, that viewing was associated with very high levels of relaxation, passivity, and non-excited moods. Further, at times when they were *not* viewing TV, the typically heavy viewers felt less concentration, less sense of control, less relaxation, and less positive moods than did lighter viewers. Kubey and Csikszentmihalyi surmised that heavy viewers are especially prone to feeling anxious and uncomfortable when alone with nothing to do. So when they are aimless and alone, TV blunts heavy viewers' negative moods and imposes a structure of sorts on their time.

Like Himmelweit et al. and Schramm et al., Kubey and Csikszentmihalyi suggest that a preexisting psychological state makes some people especially likely to gravitate to TV for the relief of discomfort and, in addition, that heavy viewing will not improve the preexisting problem and may even make it worse. In sum, three groups of serious scholars who have written about TV addiction—or heavy viewing—all agree that some people are especially vulnerable to over-involvement with TV and that if they indulge this vulnerability they may actually deepen whatever problems they had to begin with.

But let's return now to the question of whether the term "addiction" is really applicable here. Would "strong habit" perhaps be a better label? "Dependency?" In addressing this question we can benefit from a recent analysis by Robert Kubey.

Addiction, Heavy Viewing, or Dependency?

In 1996 Kubey directly addressed the comparability of "addiction" to TV and other addictions. In doing so, he relied on diagnostic criteria published in the *Diagnostic and Statistical Manual* (4th ed.) of the American Psychiatric Association (1994). Known as the *DSM-IV*, this manual for diagnosing mental disorders does not have a category called "addiction;" it instead uses the term "substance dependence." Alcoholism, for example, would come under the category of substance dependence.

In order to be labeled "substance dependent," an individual must manifest—within a 12-month period—three or more of the following characteristics:

1. *tolerance*, as defined by needing increased amounts of the substance to get the desired effect *or* a noticeably diminished effect if continuing to use the same amount of the substance;
2. *withdrawal*, as revealed by a set of symptoms that characterize withdrawal from the particular substance *or* substitution of another substance so as to avoid withdrawal symptoms;
3. frequently taking more of the substance than originally intended or using it for a longer period of time than originally intended;
4. long-standing desire to cut back or control use of the substance, which may have involved failed attempts to cut back;
5. spending a lot of time procuring, using, or recovering from using the substance;
6. curtailing important social, job-related, or leisure activities because of using the substance;
7. continuing to use the substance in spite of the knowledge that it is causing physical or psychological problems.

Recall that only *three* of these criteria must be met for a diagnosis of substance dependence. Kubey felt that five of the seven are especially relevant to television dependence—numbers 2 through 6. In the case of *withdrawal* (characteristic # 2), he pointed to a study done by Winick (1988). Winick contacted families whose TVs were broken and had been sent out for repair. He found that such families typically experienced anxiety, aggression, boredom, and irritability during withdrawal from television. Regarding # 3, Kubey pointed to numerous anecdotal reports of people watching more TV than they plan to. ESM data also hint that people may become less likely to turn off the set the longer they have been watching it. As to # 4, Kubey asserted that people quite commonly report that their efforts to cut viewing time are not successful. Some even resort to disabling the set in order to break the viewing habit. Number 5, which refers to the habit's taking a lot of time, has been amply documented by Kubey's own research using the ESM. And # 6—the curtailing of social and leisure activities—has also been demonstrated in a number of the studies that we covered in Chapter 2.

Kubey also made the point that ESM data show that TV relaxes people quickly, very shortly after they turn it on. Viewers therefore come to associate the act of turning on the television with relaxation. Interestingly, this is also a quality associated with addictive drugs. They work rapidly and their users quickly learn to associate the act of taking them with pleasure. In a sense, television becomes a readily available "quick fix" for people chronically in need of relaxation. In fact, young children often do turn to TV as a strategy for dealing with negative emotional states (Masters, Ford, & Arend, 1983).

Kubey concluded that the *DSM-IV* criteria for substance dependence apply to television use for many people. Although we may not be accustomed to thinking of TV as a "substance," Kubey pointed out that—like a drink or a drug—it does involve "taking something into the body" (1996, p. 232). What we take in, of course, are patterns of light and sound—images and words.

Development of a Dependency: A Hypothetical Scenario

Consider the experiences of a hypothetical girl. Say she was born into a home in which there was love, but little in the way of material resources. Her parents, although poorly educated, were hard-working, well-intentioned, and dedicated to the educational betterment of all their children. The girl was very shy and anxious in social situations. The television, which was on many hours a day throughout her childhood, was in the family living room—the same room in which the children usually played. Like other viewers, the little girl frequently shifted her attention back and forth from her toys to the TV. But, showing attentional inertia, she often experienced long periods of intense focus on the television screen.

As she grew older and went to school she learned how stressful the classroom, recess, and the walk home from school could be for a person as shy as she. She did not talk about her anxieties, she just felt them privately. She knew that when she got home and turned on the TV she would feel relaxed. She began to understand the programs better and to spend hours each day losing herself in the fantasy world of television. Because she did well enough in her studies, her family was not concerned about her excessive TV watching. She seldom played with other children unless the playing involved watching television.

She reached high school with her shyness and anxieties intact. People thought of her as a nice but shy girl whom they did not know very well. Her grades were good enough that she was accepted into a college a couple of hours' drive from her family's home. She arrived at college with little more social acumen than she had had in elementary school. She roomed with another girl from her high school. As the demands of college inevitably began to make themselves apparent, the girl—now a young woman—felt more anxious than ever. She reacted by redoubling her efforts to escape from reality.

We leave it to the reader to finish the story from here. Surely there is a possibility that insight, inspiration, a good friend, or a wonderful teacher will intervene to help this young woman overcome the social and emotional impoverishment of her childhood. But the deck has been stacked against her. The ready escape of television—so accessible to so many children—stood in the way of this young person's dealing with problems that really needed to be addressed. Had she been able to confront them, she might have been quite a different person by the time she went off to college.

Concluding Thoughts

Although we might surely wish for additional empirical evidence, a case can be made that over-use of television sometimes approaches the levels of dependency that we see in alcoholism or drug addiction. There is, then, some support for remarks made by the no-TV parents regarding the issue of addiction.

A question that still lingers is why some viewers and not others fall into a dependency on television. Certainly there are clues in the studies we have examined in this chapter. Predisposing characteristics may include insecurity, rejection by peers, shyness, submissiveness, being easily bored, finding reality to be aversive, a low sense of being in control, and/or anxiety and discomfort when alone with nothing to do. It may turn out that the more of these characteristics an individual possesses, the more likely he or she will be to develop a dependency. Each characteristic may constitute a single risk factor, and as such factors accumulate the risk of addiction may increase.

Another question that has not been addressed directly by scientific investigation relates to the beliefs of two of our no-TV parents —that particular children may be generally vulnerable to addictions and that allowing them access to television during childhood could increase that vulnerability. At this point, we would characterize this notion as a plausible hypothesis. We say this for two reasons. First, recall that three separate research groups (those headed by Himmelweit, Schramm, and Kubey) all expressed concern that watching large amounts of TV would prevent heavy-viewing children from developing the interpersonal skills and coping mechanisms in which they were already weak. Such youngsters' desire to flee from reality may be continued into adulthood (a time when it might manifest itself in dependence on alcohol or other drugs). Second, some studies have found correlations between heavy TV use and alcohol and drug use in teenaged boys (Tucker, 1985, 1987). So there is some justification for linking dependence on television with use of drugs and alcohol. Clearly, we haven't enough information at this point to say for sure what role, if any, television plays in the development of adult addictions. But the no-TV parents who had this thought may be onto something. Only additional research will be able to confirm whether their suspicions are true.

In the meantime, television dependency in and of itself is an issue that merits additional scientific scrutiny, if only because it has the potential to affect so many children. There are surely many ways of dealing with it in the absence of complete information; getting rid of television is but one of them.

Chapter 5

Television and Thinking

I think these kids are better off.... I don't know how they'd
be with a television, but I think their attention span is better.

– Ben Lott

[TV] is not requiring you to do any kind of thinking.... You
just sit and take it in.

– Barbara Field

You're just a receiver.... It's all just one-way.

– Nelson Field

I don't think television is any substitute for teaching. I don't
think that it communicates. I mean it washes over you.

– Adam Lake

[Television] moves on. It doesn't...wait for you to think it
out.

– Barbara Field

[When watching TV] you don't analyze and weigh things.
And so when you're presented with information that's
not...spoon-fed to you, you just don't get anything out of it.

– Barbara Field

We have a communication revolution and there's all this
information...but it's...in such a form that nobody's taking it

in. What they're carrying in their heads is much less than
what people used to carry in their heads.

– Adam Lake

Several of the no-TV parents express the belief that television
can have an effect on viewers' thinking, or cognition. Studying cognition
is not easy, of course; it must generally rely on indirect measures of
mental processes, and this inevitably introduces a degree of uncertainty
into attempts at understanding them. Nevertheless, a number of
researchers have felt that, even with the inherent uncertainties, cognition
is a topic well worth studying in the context of the television experience.

There tends to be basic agreement among cognitivists that
humans are *active* and *selective* in their ways of perceiving and thinking
about the world around them. In other words, what one focuses on and
how one makes sense of what one focuses on differ from one person to
another. We each construct a unique view of the world. Factors like
inborn talents, age, prior experiences, and current states (such as being
drowsy or in ill health) all influence our understanding of the world—our
cognitive interpretation of it. So a 2-year-old, a 12-year-old, and a 22-
year-old could all engage in the same activity—attending a church service,
say—and each would be likely to react to it and interpret it in quite a
different way. As you read this chapter, keep in mind the notion of
people as active and selective perceivers and thinkers.

It will also be helpful to be aware of what are called the *formal
features* of television. These are technological events that have been
referred to as the "syntax of television" (Huston & Wright, 1998, p. 1020)
because they mark occurrences like time shifts, changes in setting, mood
changes, or the beginnings and endings of scenes. Among other things,
formal features include zooms, cuts, fades, music, laugh tracks, and
instant replays. Formal features are of interest to us here because of their
relationship to cognition. For example, research has shown that before
the age of 6 or 7 children typically think that instant replays are real
repetitions of actions (Rice, Huston, & Wright, 1986). So just as very
young children interpret a church service differently from an adult, so too
do they interpret instant replays differently. We cannot take for granted
that formal features that seem clear and obvious to adults will be similarly
clear or obvious to children.

Methodological Considerations

In order to evaluate the no-TV parents' ideas regarding television and thinking, we need evidence of the effects of television on children's thought. The fact that measures of cognition must generally be indirect means that researchers can fairly easily pick up extraneous sources of variability in their measurement—in addition to the particular cognitive measure in which they are interested. Because a measure isn't entirely "pure," it may appear to be more watered-down and less dramatic than it would if one could measure it directly. This makes it more difficult than would otherwise be the case to demonstrate that something—like, say, television—affects thinking. In spite of the indirect, inferential quality of cognitive data, there have been successful attempts to show a relationship between TV viewing and cognitive measures.

Even if one could directly measure cognition, however, it still would be difficult to examine the effects of television viewing on children's thinking. Another inherent problem has its genesis in the ubiquity of television in our society. As we have seen, nearly every North American child grows up in a home with TV. Those who wish to study the effect of TV on thinking have nearly always been forced into studying groups of children all of whom are regular TV viewers. A no-TV comparison group is not, for most practical purposes, a realistic prospect. Since the 1960s, children being raised without television have been too few in number to be included as a comparison group in most studies.

Why make an issue of this? You will find, as we get into the topics below, that a certain degree of controversy exists among researchers regarding television's effects on thinking. Some of the controversy may occur simply because most studies do not have a no-TV comparison group. If light viewers and heavy viewers are compared on a cognitive variable and are found not to differ greatly, the deduction is often made that TV simply does not exert much influence on that variable. However, the lack of a difference between viewers with different television diets *could* occur because "light" and "heavy" viewing affect thinking in similar ways. Maybe it does not take much regular TV watching to influence thinking. Perhaps the big change in thinking happens between 0 hours of viewing per week and 5 hours per week, rather than between 10 and 20 hours. Few studies address this issue.

So there are two problems, both of which have the potential to diminish the visibility of television's effects on thinking. First, it is difficult to get a direct, uncontaminated measure of many cognitive variables and, as a result, they may appear to be weaker than would be the case if one could access them directly. Second, researchers often have to get along without a no-TV comparison group; but even with a relatively weak cognitive variable, a no-TV comparison might make it possible to demonstrate a reliable effect of television—if, in fact, such an effect exists.

We have to be cautious, then, in interpreting findings and drawing conclusions. An error in *either* direction—toward concluding TV is not all that bad or toward concluding it is a danger to children—would be a step off the path to truth. And that, of course, is a digression that science seeks to avoid. With this in mind, we turn to a consideration of how television may—or may not—influence attention span.

Attention Span or Persistence

Attention span typically refers to the length of time a person can stay focused on a single activity or event. Generally, it is to a child's advantage to have a fairly long attention span—though attention, like all good things, could be carried to a pathological extreme. But within normal limits, children tend to be better off if they can stay focused on an arithmetic problem, say for 5 minutes, rather than if their attention wanders after just a few seconds or a minute. The important thing is that they persist at the task until they have completed it.

Television often gets blamed for the shortened attention spans that are perceived to exist in many youngsters today. Many educators and parents believe that fast-paced, rapidly-changing television presentations keep children from developing the habit of deploying their attention in a persistent and focused way. Whether TV is, in fact, at fault when children have difficulty sticking to their work has been a matter of scientific debate. In one review of the scientific literature, Anderson and Collins (1988) discovered conflicting evidence regarding how television influences attention span. Any effect, these authors concluded, may depend on the type of television shows children watch. Violent action shows may stimulate shorter attention spans, while educational programs may actually make children more persistent.

Whatever turns out to be the case, it is not likely that we will find an entirely simple relationship between the pacing of TV programs and children's subsequent attention spans. In one study, two versions of *Sesame Street* were created—one very fast-paced and the other very slow-paced. Preschoolers who had seen the slow-paced show were no more persistent after viewing it than were children who had seen the fast-paced show (Anderson, Levin, & Lorch, 1977). It is possible, of course, that attention span is one of those variables that is influenced by *long*-term exposure to television. If this is the case, a short-term exposure to one particular program probably will not have much effect on children who have already watched thousands of hours of TV at home. This, then, is one of the situations in which a group of no-TV children would be very useful for comparison purposes.

Another investigation involved longer-term exposure to a particular television stimulus and, like the *Sesame Street* study, included a measure of preschool children's attention spans (Friedrich & Stein, 1973). For 4 weeks during a summer nursery program, youngsters in this study saw videos of one of three types of program: shows designed to teach and to foster harmonious human relationships (episodes of *Mister Rogers' Neighborhood*), aggressive shows (*Batman* and *Superman* cartoons), or neutral programs. Children who watched *Mr. Rogers* for 4 weeks ended up with longer attention spans than those who had seen neutral shows; those who watched the aggressive cartoons had shorter attention spans than the neutral program group. With a longer-term experimental treatment, then, TV's effects on persistence were measurable.

Some relevant data from a no-TV sample were collected during a study of a Canadian town that did not get television reception until the mid-1970s. Investigators were able to study the citizens of the town (dubbed "Notel") before television came on the scene and, again, 2 years after its arrival. On both occasions comparisons were made to two other, demographically similar towns—one that had reception of a single TV station ("Unitel") and one that received four channels ("Multitel"). During the course of this study, many measures were taken on both children and adults. Included among the measures taken on adults was a measure of persistence. The adults were presented with a difficult problem-solving task and researchers noted how long they worked at the problem before giving up. Before TV came to Notel, its adult residents persisted at the problem task for an average of 401 seconds before giving up. Those from Unitel kept trying for 280 seconds and Multitel residents tried for 332 seconds. The Notelians were significantly more persistent than those from towns with TV. Interestingly, these differences were still in evidence 2 years after the introduction of television in Notel. Again Notel adults persisted significantly longer at trying to solve a problem than did people from Unitel and Multitel (MacBeth, 1996; Suedfeld, Little, Rank, Rank, & Ballard, 1986).

The fact that persistence survived in the Notel citizenry after the coming of television is a hopeful sign, suggesting that persistence, once established, may be a fairly durable human characteristic (MacBeth, 1996). Its limits have by no means been tested, however. And the fact that the no-TV group was composed of adults gives us little to go on in speculating about how children might react. The scientific record is, at this point, incomplete. The no-TV parents who believe their children have longer attention spans as a result of not having television may be right, but scientific evidence in support of that opinion awaits further research.

Mental Effort and Concentration

If it does turn out to be the case that television viewing reliably limits viewers' attention spans, then we will probably begin to wonder about the mechanism or route by which this comes about. A likely candidate, we suspect, will be the amount of mental effort or concentration typically required to watch TV. If little mental effort is required, then viewers are in effect being trained, whenever they are watching, to put forth minimal effort. The more they watch TV, the more such training they receive.

Some of our no-TV parents expressed just this belief—that watching TV does not require much in the way of mental effort. As it happens, researchers have addressed this issue and have come up with some intriguing findings. Interest in the topic can be traced in part to Gavriel Salomon's (1983) notion of Amount of Invested Mental Effort (AIME), which suggests that viewers learn more from presentations in which they invest more mental effort.

One group of investigators (Kerkman, Piñon, Wright, & Huston, 1996) reasoned that U.S. children, with a long history of watching entertainment television, have learned that TV is easy to understand, nondemanding, and fun. Youngsters consequently may go into a low-effort mode when they watch any TV program, even an educational one. In this study, children were presented with a problem that has been used before in studying cognitive development—a balance scale problem (Siegler, 1978). The balance scale is a miniature seesaw with pegs sticking up at intervals on either side of the central fulcrum. The scale is held immobile while weights are placed on various pegs and the child is asked in which direction, if either, it will tip if it is allowed to swing freely. By soliciting children's predictions of tilt and their explanations for their predictions, one can gain insight into the sophistication of their thinking.

Kerkman and colleagues presented 5- and 7-year-olds with balance scale problems either live—before their very eyes—or on videotape. Half the children saw the live version first and then the video version; the other half saw the video followed by the live presentation. When children saw the live version first, many of them figured out and solved the balance scale problems correctly. Then, when the same youngsters were next shown the video version, they were equally sophisticated at solving problems presented that way. The results were different, however, for youngsters who saw the video problems first. These children used a less successful, less sophisticated approach to solving them. When next shown the live problems, their performance was better—on a par with children in the other group.

So order of presentation mattered. If "live" experience came first, it seemed to pave the way to accuracy on the video problems. If video came first, it was approached in a less cognitively sophisticated way. Why should this be? The investigators felt that Salomon's notion of mental effort offers a plausible explanation for their results. Five- and seven-year-olds, already having experienced hundreds (and perhaps thousands) of hours of entertainment television, had developed the attitude that "TV is easy" (Kerkman et al., 1996, p. 239). If they had not had the focusing, effortful experience of solving live balance scale problems first, they reacted to them on the TV screen as problems that do not require diligent effort. And they failed to solve them. Even though they had the ability to solve them, they did not.

According to this line of reasoning, then, TV—in its present incarnation as a predominantly entertainment medium—makes child viewers, and perhaps the rest of us as well, mentally lazy, at least when it comes to video presentations. It is heartening that "laziness" on video balance scale problems was reversible under live circumstances. But many questions remain as to just how far the view that "TV is easy" might generalize, and whether cumulative experiences with TV as children get older might deepen the effect. At this point we have some provocative clues, but there is much yet to be understood.

Before leaving the topic of mental effort, let's take a brief look at some more data gathered by Kubey and Csikszentmihalyi (1990) using the Experience Sampling Method (ESM). Each time participants (all adults) in this study were beeped, they filled out forms that included questions on their level of *concentration*.

True to the "TV is easy" notion implied by the research just described, Kubey and Csikszentmihalyi found that people reported less concentration during TV viewing than during other leisure activities. Further, when the researchers looked at prolonged periods of TV-watching, they found that levels of concentration dropped even lower as people continued to watch. This pattern was different from that seen during other prolonged activities. During long periods of reading, for example, concentration increased over time. As you might expect, as levels of concentration dropped, people also found it more *difficult* to concentrate. This difficulty in focusing persisted even after participants had turned off the TV and were doing something else. (On the other hand, they had less difficulty concentrating on another activity after reading periods.) Kubey and Csikszentmihalyi (1990) concluded that watching television is a "low-involvement activity" and that, paradoxically, "low cognitive effort by the viewer may make it harder, not easier, to continue concentrating" (p. 135).

The no-TV parents who believe that television watching requires little mental effort can find support for their opinion in the scientific literature. We must keep in mind, however, that the findings to date are sparse and that they refer to television as it is currently configured—as a medium predominantly used for entertainment. The studies mentioned here would have to be redone if television suddenly became predominantly educational or informational. We believe the chances of such a change are slim, for reasons we will address in Chapter 7. But, theoretically at least, the possibility exists.

Fantasy and Imaginative Play

A key feature of human thinking is the ability to speculate, to fantasize, to imagine, to dream. This capacity to entertain possibilities may set us apart from other animals and it surely enriches our lives. Not only does it provide absorbing, emotionally rewarding moments, but it also occasionally helps us specify goals that have a salutary impact on the real circumstances of our lives.

Young Isaac Greenwald surely expressed a positive evaluation of fantasy when he listed day dreaming as his favorite leisure activity. Although none of the no-TV parents mentioned fantasy or imaginative play in so many words, they commonly expressed a desire for their children to be flexible and resourceful. On the assumption that a good imagination and capacity for fantasy may contribute significantly to flexibility and resourcefulness, let's take a brief look at what scientific investigations have yielded regarding the relationship between television and imaginative play behavior.

Several scholars have reviewed the research literature on television and imaginative play. The reviews are limited by the fact that most studies have involved preschool children and have looked only at short-term effects of television on young children's creative play (van der Voort & Valkenburg, 1994). To complicate matters further, there have been some contradictory findings within the existing literature. Despite these limiting conditions, the majority of reviewers have concluded that evidence for TV's having an adverse effect on creativity is stronger than evidence for no effect or for a positive impact (see Greenfield et al., 1993; MacBeth, 1996; Singer, 1993; Singer & Singer, 1983; van der Voort & Valkenberg, 1994). In one dissenting review, Anderson and Collins (1988) concluded that there is little evidence that TV has any effect on creativity. The negative impact of television on creative play seems to be especially noticeable or pronounced when the TV programming to which study participants have been exposed is of the high action, aggressive type. Occasionally, educational programs specifically designed to encourage fantasy play have been shown to result in increased creativity.

A particularly interesting feature of the fantasy lives of many young children is the *imaginary playmate*. Singer and Singer (1981) studied this phenomenon in a group of middle class preschoolers. They found that 65% of these children had created fantasy friends. Those who had done so tended to be happier and more cooperative and to use richer language during school play times than youngsters who did not have imaginary playmates. Of special interest to us is the finding that children with imaginary friends watched less television than the other children.

It is possible, of course, that a child's fantasy life may influence his or her selections of TV programming. It seems equally plausible that limiting TV viewing and providing interesting activities would give a child more time and more mental wherewithal for creative play activities. As we have noted before, a large sample of no-TV children would be an instructive comparison group.

Creative Problem-Solving

Creativity in older children and adults changes from the play behavior of early childhood to include many other types of behaviors, a number of which might be categorized as intellectual activities that involve sizing up and solving problems. Although we might wish for more ample and conclusive evidence, there have been some instructive findings as to the relationship between TV and creativity in older age groups. Let's look at evidence from the "Notel" study we described earlier (MacBeth, 1996; Williams, 1986). It is of particular interest because it assessed creativity in both children and adults and, most especially, because it incorporated the highly desirable no-TV comparison group.

Children's creativity was measured using the Alternate Uses task, which was designed as a test of *ideational fluency*—the ability to produce multiple creative ideas. On this test, each child is asked to list as many different uses as he or she can think of for a variety of common objects (such as a knife or a magazine). During the first phase of the study (before TV came to Notel), fourth and seventh graders in all three towns (Notel, Unitel, and Multitel) took the Alternate Uses Test. The test was given again to these same children during Phase 2, 2 years after Notel had gotten TV. The youngsters were by then sixth and ninth graders. A group of new fourth and seventh graders was also tested during Phase 2.

In Phase 1, the only time when a no-TV comparison group was available, Notel's children scored significantly higher than youngsters from both Unitel and Multitel on the Alternate Uses Test. By Phase 2, however, Notel's children—both those being retested and the new participants—had dropped to the Unitel/Multitel level (Harrison & Williams, 1986). This result bolsters the belief that living without television may foster creativity. On the basis of additional evidence gathered in the course of the study, the investigators speculated that Notel children were more creative before TV because they engaged in—and were enriched by—a greater variety of activities. As they cut back on these activities once they had TV to occupy their time, their creativity was blunted. Thus, TV viewing may be at least indirectly associated with declines in children's creativity.

Creative problem-solving in adults was also tested in the three towns before Notel had television (Suedfeld et al., 1986). Adults were given the Duncker candle problem, which requires participants to use a set of materials in an unusual and creative way in order to solve a problem. The problem is moderately difficult and, typically, not all adults are able to solve it. Interestingly, 40.4% of Notel adults solved it, whereas only 25.5% of Unitel residents and 30% of Multitel residents did so.

In Unitel and Multitel, those who solved the problem watched TV an average of 18.1 hours per week; those who could not solve the problem watched an average of 33.4 hours in a week. But if you are thinking that watching smaller amounts of TV is probably equivalent to having no TV at all, consider the following: People who solved the problem in Notel did so in 151 seconds, on average. Unitelians who solved it took an average of 251 seconds and Multitel solvers averaged 263 seconds. As a group, the Notel adults before TV were sharper and quicker at this test of creative problem-solving.

It would be interesting to know whether the creativity differences remained or disappeared after Notel got TV. Unfortunately, the test that was given to adults during Phase 2 proved so difficult that virtually no one could solve it and it was thus an ineffective measure of creativity. The question of whether television's coming would blunt adult creative problem-solving remains unanswered.

Kubey and Csikszentmihalyi (1990) have noted that solutions to personal and societal problems do not come easily to human beings. Solutions require concentrated use of mental energy. TV may drain off some of the energy we could be putting to use in more creative ways. Remember our conservative estimate of 2½ hours per day—17½ hours per week—of television use for the average person? Surely there are any number of problems that might benefit from additional attention if some of those person-hours were put to different use.

Unreflective Viewing

Some of our no-TV parents were expressly concerned about television's incompatibility with reflective, analytic thought. They have not been alone in this concern and scholars have sought to discover just how intellectually passive TV watchers really are during viewing.

Anderson and colleagues (Anderson, Alwitt, Lorch, & Levin, 1979; Anderson & Lorch, 1983), using the technique of watching children as they watched TV, concluded that youngsters are active and selective in shifting their attention to and away from TV. Children are responsive to the formal features of television at a young age and use those features to help them grasp the central messages in televised material. They appear to choose when to attend to TV based on the comprehensibility of program content and its interest value for them. The hardiness of such findings has prompted some experts in the field to declare that "most scholars have abandoned the stereotyped notion that television induces passive, mindless states" (Huston & Wright, 1998, p. 1000).

To cap debate at this point, however, would shirk the no-TV parents' concern that televised information "washes over" the viewer without allowing time to "think it out." Indeed, we can accept that viewers are active and selective in allocating their attention and still wonder whether the relentless pace of televised information allows adequate time for reflection (Singer & Singer, 1983).

Among cognitively-oriented psychologists, there is general agreement that as we process incoming information we tend to rehearse (or repeat) it and mentally organize it into categories that relate it to what we already know. Rehearsing and organizing help us to remember the information as well as to determine its relevance to our lives and concerns. Not surprisingly, these processes take time. We can take in and store huge amounts of information, but we must do so at a finite pace.

Singer and Singer (1983) have suggested that the pace of televised information—especially on children's programs—does not allow children time to reflect. Apart from the purely cognitive implications of this, the Singers believe fast-paced TV may actually generate an aroused, unpleasant *emotional* state as well. In fact, in their research they found a positive correlation between heavy viewing of fast-paced shows and children's aggressive behavior (Singer & Singer, 1980, 1981). In other words, youngsters who watched more fast-paced programming than their peers also tended to be the most aggressive children in the group. This finding held even after the effects of aggressive content in the shows had been removed from the calculations.

In contrast to many (not all) educational children's programs, commercially-produced programs are faster-paced (Condry, 1989). Use of formal features that might permit reflection is quite limited (Huston et al., 1981). Rather, the features used—animation, slapstick humor, strange noises and video effects—seem to be designed in the belief that the viewer must be captured and held by an unrelenting stream of attention-getting devices (Condry, 1989). And it seems to work. Highly popular children's programs incorporate many such features (Wright et al., 1984).

So formal features that interfere with reflective thought are, at the same time, often alluring to the mass audience. This may be putting television on a collision course with what is best for children—at least as far as their ability to think and reflect is concerned. Even the often-praised *Sesame Street*, which was modeled in part on successful commercial programming, may encourage unreflective viewing (Singer & Singer, 1983). At the present time there is too little empirical evidence on reflection during TV viewing to make a definitive statement. At best, we can say that the parents who have chosen to raise their children without television *may* be right about this issue.

Missing Information

Before leaving the topic of television's influence on cognitive activities and abilities, let's consider for a moment the nature of televised information. Can one learn about anything one wants to know by watching television, provided one is selective and patient enough? If you have full-service cable and a recorder is the *whole world* then available to you via your TV screen? A few moments of reflection will probably convince you that the answer to both questions is "no." To explore this matter further, consider the provocative work of Bill McKibben (1992).

McKibben is a journalist, not a scientist. Scientists, who seek inspiration for their work from many sources, may find several of McKibben's ideas worthy of additional research. He set out to compare a day of television with a day spent camping, hiking, and swimming near his home in the Adirondack mountains. For the "television" day, he procured videotapes of everything broadcast on every cable and broadcast channel in Fairfax, Virginia for one day in May, 1990. He ended up with over 1000 hours of videotape. And he watched it *all*. His book, *The Age of Missing Information*, summarizes the insights he gained from comparing the 1000+ hours of television with the 24 hours he spent alone on the mountain.

Generally, McKibben was impressed with the very narrow band of information that makes suitable subject matter for television. Take nature, for example—one of the topics that he writes about most compellingly. During his day "in nature," he found that all his senses were stimulated. He was cold, hot, wet, sore, relaxed. His body was exercised. Various emotions were stimulated. There was little if any drama during his day of hiking but, rather, his appreciation of the complex interplay of vast, ancient biological, geological, and meteorological systems was reaffirmed.

These experiences were very different from the view of nature that was cabled and beamed into Fairfax on that May day. One thing that McKibben noticed was that only a few species really met the requirements to be featured on TV. If species are particularly cute *or* ugly, if they are very friendly *or* ferocious, if they live in an accessible location, and if they are the "correct size to show up well on camera" (McKibben, 1992, p. 77), then they might get to star in a nature documentary or a news story.

In addition to showing a narrow range of species, nature television also focused on a narrow range of events—often very dramatic ones, such as predator-prey encounters or mating displays. McKibben appreciates that these things do happen in nature, but he argues that TV makes it look as if they happen all the time when, in fact, they are relatively rare occurrences. He likens this phenomenon to looking at the highlights of a basketball game rather than the game itself. Left out of television's picture almost entirely were those vast, interacting systems of nature that McKibben was so aware of during his real day in nature. As he summarizes it, "The upshot of a nature education by television is a deep fondness for certain species and a deep lack of understanding of systems, or of the policies that destroy those systems" (McKibben, 1992, p. 79).

In addition to television's subject matter being narrowed to "televisable" content, McKibben also feels that the nonstop pace of the medium limits what the viewer is able to do with the information that is there. In a memorable passage on the topic he writes:

> If God decided to deliver the Ten Commandments on the *Today* show, it's true he'd have an enormous audience. But the minute he was finished, or maybe after he'd gotten through six or seven, it would be time for a commercial and then a discussion with a pet psychiatrist about how to introduce your dog to your new baby (McKibben, 1992, p. 216).

Concluding Thoughts

To conclude the chapter, let's quickly review the findings we have examined. There is a need for additional research in all areas, but the current shape of the findings suggests that

- television can shorten attention span or persistence, particularly after long-term exposure to the medium;
- television, which at present serves primarily an entertainment function, requires relatively little of its viewers in terms of mental effort or concentration;
- television—especially high action, aggressive programming— may dampen young children's creative play behavior;
- television may blunt creative problem-solving in older children and adults; and
- there is reason to suspect that the cascade of fast-paced programming that typifies contemporary television may hamper reflective thought during viewing.

The pattern of results suggests that television does impose some cognitive limitations on its viewers. Further, the medium itself is limited with regard to the type of information it can and does convey. Many parents who are aware of these dual limitations may encourage their children not to overindulge their appetites for television. Some may simply opt not to have a TV at all.

Chapter 6

Reading and Watching

[Television] washes over you.... The written word requires a kind of commitment because it requires...effort. So you read it and you've made a mental effort.

– Adam Lake

I...read...Christina at least 100 books before she was one.... We...read little kids' books...practically from the time she could hold her head up.

– Joellen Stelling

I read to the children at least 30 minutes a day and maybe twice that because it may be in the morning and at night.... They just adore books.

– Joellen Stelling

They were both real early talkers and people thought that that was remarkable—their vocabulary.

– Joellen Stelling

My son reads much more than most children [his] age.... By the time he had turned 12 he'd read all the kids' classics...all of Mark Twain and all of...*The Lord of the Rings*.

– Eve Greenwald

You have children who are in third grade and they can't read.... I mean, it's a national problem.... We need the...guardians of these children to do their job.

> – Dave Stelling

I always carry reading material and utilize waiting time or break/lunch time.

> – Barbara Field

I read every day, whenever I have a free moment or down time. (Car pooling presents many such opportunities.) I also read every night before sleep and many mornings on waking.

> – Laura Lott

Our no-TV parents express few specific beliefs regarding the relationship between television use and reading, but it is clear from their actions that they value reading highly. They read a lot themselves, they encourage reading in their children, and they make frequent use of public libraries. As a group, their own academic accomplishments are considerable. Of the eight parents, seven have education beyond high school and two hold doctoral degrees. They have an abiding interest in the academic progress of their offspring. It can easily be argued, on the basis of both behaviors and attitudes, that these parents see reading as a fundamental and indispensable skill. Unstated—but implied—is their belief that television in the home would be an impediment to reading.

In this chapter we will examine the relationship between TV-viewing and reading—a topic that has been a focus of scientific scrutiny since the early days of television. The topic embodies complexities that have made it difficult to study, but researchers have persevered in their attempts to shine light on the subject.

Research on the television/reading relationship takes place in a context of general cultural concern about young people's reading. Declining reading achievement has been a matter of national concern since the 1970s (Beentjes & van der Voort, 1988). In fact, from the mid-1970s to the early 1990s there was a steady decline in the percentage of high school seniors who characterize themselves as daily readers of books, magazines, or newspapers. Whereas about 60% of seniors were daily readers in the late 1970s, only about 45% were by the late 1980s (Glenn, 1994). And an astonishing 14% of U.S. eighth graders are unable to accomplish basic reading tasks (Hafner, Ingels, Schneider, & Stevenson, 1990). Vocabulary size appears to be declining across successive generations at all educational levels (Glenn, 1994). For those who value reading, there is reason for concern. Large numbers of young citizens are either going without the information available in books, magazines, and newspapers or are gaining access to it in some alternative —possibly inferior—way.

It is awfully easy to blame television for these reading problems. Just the discrepancy between time spent reading and time spent watching TV would cause even a casual observer to raise an eyebrow. For example, a group of Illinois fifth graders who kept time diaries reported watching TV an average of 131.1 minutes per day and reading only 18.4 minutes. The reading figure included reading books, comics, newspapers, magazines, and the mail and represented reading that occurred during out-of-school hours (Anderson, Wilson, & Fielding, 1988). U.S. eighth graders, on average, spend 4 times more time watching TV than working on homework (Hafner et al., 1990). Nearly 90% of college-level communications teachers and researchers surveyed by Bybee, Robinson, and Turon (1982, cited in Comstock, 1991) saw TV as one of the causes of decreased reading.

So there seems to be a reading decline, which many view as a problem, in the U.S. And the problem came along at roughly the same time in history that television was achieving its full infiltration into U.S. homes. But such a coincidence does not constitute proof that TV is causing children to read less. In fact, the inability to specify a cause has been a persistent source of uncertainty in research on television and reading.

Studies During Television's Introduction

In one of the earliest studies of television and children, Eleanor Maccoby (1951) interviewed a large, representative sample of families with and without television sets in Cambridge, Massachusetts. She found that children in homes with TV did substantially less recreational reading than youngsters in no-TV homes. The children in television homes also did less homework than no-TV children, but this difference occurred mainly on Sundays and not on weekdays.

Himmelweit, Oppenheim, and Vince (1958), in their study of British school children, reported that when TV was first acquired by families, their children's reading—especially book reading—declined. Later, after about 3 years with television, book reading rebounded to its earlier level. Often children's reading choices reflected things they had seen on television. It was the view of Himmelweit and her colleagues that television actually encouraged more reading than would otherwise occur in children of average intelligence.

Both Maccoby (1951) and Himmelweit et al. (1958) noted that the first wave of families to acquire TVs tended to be less "bookish" in orientation than the families who waited a while before buying a television. In Maccoby's study, it was the more highly educated professional families who were skeptical about television's worth and who put off obtaining a set. In the British study, families who got TV earlier tended to favor reading more comic books and "less mature" (Himmelweit et al., 1958, pp. 324-325) books and periodicals than those who acquired their TVs later. Such findings raise the possibility that observed reading declines in TV children might be due to family influences rather than to television itself.

Schramm, Lyle, and Parker (1961), studying the introduction of TV in the U.S., found book, magazine, and newspaper use to be unchanged after the acquisition of television. Comic book reading, however, did decline after TV came into the home. So too did reading of lesser-quality magazines (such as confession and screen magazines). Comic book reading was substantially lower in TV homes for all age groups studied (first, sixth, and tenth graders). Also, sixth and tenth graders with TV did about 15 minutes less homework per night than did their age mates who did not have TV. Echoing the observation of the two previous studies, Schramm et al. (1961) noted that the reading habits of youngsters in this study tended to reflect the educational and economic levels of their families, with children from more educated and affluent families reading more.

So far, then, we see that some reading declines happened in the early TV families, but we cannot tell whether they were due to those families' not encouraging reading, to television's displacing reading, or to both. We gain some additional insight from the results of a study that compared per capita library circulation rates in communities where television was available and where it was not (Parker, 1963). Data were collected during the 1950s. Communities were matched on population size and library circulation rates, as well as community type (rural or urban/suburban). If families who purchased television were people who did not read anyway, then we would expect their acquisition of TV to have little impact on library use. However, if TV really did cut into reading time, then library use would be expected to decline. In fact, the towns with television had lower use of library materials than did the towns that were yet to receive TV. Circulation reductions involved mainly works of fiction. The fact that TV-related reading declines were evident on a community-wide basis supports the argument that something in addition to family factors may have influenced the reading drop. It is possible that the something was TV.

The study of the introduction of TV to the Canadian town of Notel is of special importance because it permitted comparison of "mature" TV families, who had had television for several years, and non-users who had never lived with television. It is likely that any rebounding of early reading declines in Unitel and Multitel (the towns that had TV) would have already happened by the time this study was done. Despite this, in comparison to children from towns with television, second-graders from TV-less Notel were better readers (Corteen & Williams, 1986). This finding was accounted for mainly by the reading scores of boys. After examining all their data, the authors concluded that TV probably interferes with learning to read but once one has acquired reading skills, TV's effect on reading achievement is minimal. They speculated that TV encourages less bright children and others who have particular difficulties learning to read to drop out of the reading scene early on and rely instead on television for entertainment and information. This might result in certain children never learning to read well.

Based on the studies just described, and on others with similar findings (e.g., Hornik, 1978; Mutz, Roberts, & van Vuuren, 1993), there is some cause for concern regarding television's potential effect on children's reading. Concern would appear to focus especially on short-term "novelty" effects and on children who are just learning to read. However, additional research has revealed other issues to consider.

Correlational Studies

Once the no-TV group in society effectively had disappeared, a different kind of study became the preferred mode of investigation. This was the correlational study—in which rates of television-viewing are related to measures of reading. A correlational study allows an investigator to determine whether, across a whole group of children, TV-viewing is related to reading achievement consistently. There are basically three possible outcomes of such a study: (1) children who watch a lot of TV also have high reading achievement and low-viewing youngsters have low reading scores; (2) high TV-viewing children have low reading achievement and low-viewing children excel at reading; or (3) the two measurements are not related in any consistent way.

Early studies of this simple correlational type provided modest support for the idea that TV-viewing and reading achievement varied in opposition to one another (Beentjes & van der Voort, 1988; Desmond, 2001; Huston & Wright, 1998; MacBeth, 1996). Evidence was weak and sometimes contradictory, but there appeared to be a slight tendency for higher TV-viewing to be associated with lower reading scores. A clearer but more complex picture of the TV/reading relationship started to emerge in the 1980s when investigators began studying very large samples of children and applying more sophisticated statistical analyses to their data. Neuman (1988) analyzed data gathered from over a million public school children in eight different states. She found that, for elementary and middle school children, the relationship between TV use and reading achievement was curvilinear.

Neuman's results can be described quite simply. Children who watched no TV at all scored somewhat lower on reading achievement than youngsters who watched 2 hours a day. So for viewing at these lower levels, TV use tended to vary in parallel with reading ability; higher TV use was associated with better reading ability. The relationship was dramatically reversed, however, for children who watched 3 or more hours per day of television. When youngsters viewed at higher levels (which are often typical of modern North American children), TV use and reading achievement varied in opposition to one another; children who extended their TV viewing beyond 3 or 4 hours daily showed steep drops in reading achievement as viewing time increased.

Interestingly, the curvilinear relationship that was evident among the younger children was not displayed by the high school students in Neuman's study. For high schoolers, there was a simple, linear tendency for reading achievement to drop as TV viewing increased, across the whole range of viewing times. Similar results—for both younger and older children—were found in another study of over 77,000 9-, 13-, and 17-year-olds from across the U.S. (Searls, Mead, & Ward, 1985).

How are we to interpret such findings? To begin with, it is important to remember that correlational studies reveal relationships among different measures but they do not prove causality. The finding that increased TV use is associated with lower reading scores does not prove TV use causes poor reading skills. It leaves open this possibility, but it also leaves open two other possibilities: that poor reading causes increased TV use, or that some third factor causes both overuse of TV and poor skill at reading.

Although subject to these uncertainties of interpretation, well done correlational studies do, at least, give scholars solid facts to speculate about. In that spirit, Comstock (1991) speculated that the curvilinear pattern of results for younger children found by Neuman (1988) could come about because watching TV may actually be intellectually enriching for inexperienced children. Up to a point, TV may provide stimulation for such youngsters and thus help improve their reading. For more experienced children—such as high school students—however, TV may be more of a "deprivation" experience. Even in quite small doses it may divert them from more valuable activities and diminish their reading ability in comparison to youngsters who watch less. This interpretation has built into it a comparison between the stimulation that TV provides and the stimulation that "real life" provides. Accordingly, then, whenever parents or others are able to provide children of any age with a real life more stimulating than TV, TV would be a deterrent to developing improved reading skills.

This may explain Neuman's (1988) finding that elementary and middle school children who watched 2 hours of TV a day had somewhat higher reading abilities than children who watched no TV at all. However, it is wise to exercise caution in interpreting this finding, inasmuch as we know nothing about the no-TV children in this study. In a huge sample like Neuman's, there were undoubtedly children who reported no TV viewing for a variety of different reasons, which might have included having a broken TV set, being on restriction, being away from home, experiencing a family crisis, *or* coming from a home like the children in our no-TV families. Were we able to obtain separate reading scores for various groups of nonviewers we would likely gain additional insight as to the nature of the TV/reading relationship. For now, we can say provisionally that a little TV does not appear to impede reading ability.

Before we move on, there is an additional way of thinking about correlational findings that we would like to spotlight briefly. It relates to the "third factor" interpretation mentioned above. Perhaps the television/reading relationships that have been found in correlational studies come about through the operation of some third factor that influences both reading and watching TV. A candidate for such a third factor was hinted at in the early studies by Maccoby (1951), Himmelweit et al. (1958), and Schramm et al. (1961). Recall that researchers in all three of these studies found that families differed in the way they felt about reading and that this seemed to be related to how soon they acquired TV and how they adapted to it once they had it. Perhaps the value a family places on reading will determine how much children read *and* how much they are allowed to watch TV. In fact, Neuman (1988) speculated that the TV/reading relationships she identified might be influenced by parenting. In the next section we will address parental factors in the relationship between television use and reading skill.

Parenting, Watching, Reading, and Program Type

Several studies of parent and family variables, television use, and reading collectively suggest that a number of characteristics often occur together. To illustrate, there is a tendency for lower socioeconomic status, lower parental education, higher TV viewing (particularly of entertainment programming), and lower child reading achievement to occur as a cluster within families. Similarly, higher socioeconomic status, higher parental education, less TV viewing (favoring informational programming), and higher child reading achievement tend to occur together (California Assessment Program, 1982; Comstock, 1991; Truglio, Murphy, Oppenheimer, Huston, & Wright, 1996; Zuckerman, Singer, & Singer, 1980).

Findings such as these sharpen the focus of our emerging picture. But they are still derived from correlational studies and, as such, do not tell us which of the clustered factors, if any, are causes and which are effects. If our practical goal were to improve children's reading, we might choose to start by making changes in any of the factors. You will probably agree, however, that changing the economic and educational levels of the parents would be very time-consuming and possibly quite difficult. By comparison, it would be substantially easier to restrict television viewing and to encourage consumption of informational programs. Our no-TV families, of course, have simply cut home television consumption to zero.

Broadening the Search for Causes

Correlational studies have provided tantalizing clues as to the possible effects of television use on reading. What we would really like, though, is to go beyond the circumstantial evidence and try to find stronger verification of television's impact on reading. A Dutch study of 828 second- and fourth-graders who were followed for a 3-year period carries us a bit further in that direction (Koolstra & van der Voort, 1996; Koolstra, van der Voort, & van der Kamp, 1997). This study is still correlational, but it was designed to test various causal mechanisms that might be operating between TV use and leisure-time book reading. The investigators found that even after they statistically removed the effects of socioeconomic status and IQ from their calculations, there was still a significant tendency for more television viewing to be associated with less leisure-time book reading and lower reading comprehension. The causal linkages suggested by their pattern of findings were as follows: (1) the easy, pleasant qualities of TV viewing gradually make it preferable to books as a source of satisfaction; (2) over time, frequent use of television is associated with increased difficulty concentrating on reading; (3) there is a general devaluing of reading within the child culture; and consequently (4) there is less reading of books during leisure hours. These findings take on a certain urgency when considered in light of other research showing that book reading is the best known predictor of children's reading achievement scores (Anderson et al., 1988).

The results of the Dutch study are in keeping with Kubey and Csikszentmihalyi's (1990) finding that adults experience a greater sense of concentration and effort and a higher level of alertness while reading than while watching TV. They are also in agreement with Salomon's (1984) finding that sixth graders find TV to be easy and print to be difficult.

Reading or being read to—coping with words—is generally harder than watching TV for children and adults. For many children confronted with the choice of watching TV or reading a book, TV is the path of least resistance. But reading has the potential to be more personal and more tailored to one's preexisting store of knowledge than television. Further, the information available to us in written form is far broader in subject matter and greater in quantity than what is available on video. It speaks more directly of subjective states and provides us with connections to our human past that are simply not available via television. And as readers we can stop, ponder, skip around, and reread freely, whereas the tempo of television is essentially not within the viewer's control (Kubey & Csikszentmihalyi, 1990). Because reading is so versatile and can address such diverse subject matter, we would argue that adults have a responsibility to help children become excellent readers. Television is apt to be a deterrent to this process, especially when it is regularly watched to excess.

So far, we have been considering TV viewing and reading as two separate activities that take place at different times. But what happens when one tries to do them at the *same* time?

Television as a Background to Reading

You may remember from Chapter 2 that adults frequently share their television time with other activities. Sometimes they read with the TV on. The extent to which children do this is not really known, but some disquieting hints exist in the literature. In a survey of British television viewers, Wober (1990) found that 74% of 12- to 15-year-olds did homework and more than half of these youngsters did their homework with the TV on. California sixth graders also reported doing homework with the TV on, with heavier viewers being more likely than lighter viewers to do so (California Assessment Program, 1982).

An experimental study of college students examined the effects of background television on a variety of different tasks (Armstrong & Greenberg, 1990). The results showed that background TV led to reduced performance in three types of tasks—reading comprehension, complex problem solving, and creative thinking. The investigators concluded that "those who habitually combine homework, reading, and other intellectually demanding activities with television are likely to be getting less benefit from these activities" (Armstrong & Greenberg, 1990, p. 379). Additional research has suggested that it may be the verbal content of television that makes it especially disruptive to reading (Salame & Baddeley, 1989) and that the disruption may occur mainly through interference with memory processes (Armstrong & Sopory, 1997).

Because these investigations were experimental and not correlational in nature, they enable us to make statements about causality. Based on the evidence accumulated to date, we can say that a TV in the background does cause lower reading comprehension in the short term. If the reading-with-TV scenario is repeated over and over again, we have reason to predict long-term deficits in reading ability. Parents who care about such things will almost certainly want to encourage their children to turn off the television when reading and doing homework. Parents in homes without TV will not have to confront the issue.

Dinner Time

Each of our no-TV families regularly sits down to meals as a group. Such occasions create opportunities for exchanging information, dealing with problems, expressing emotions, and establishing family traditions. In the process, mealtime conversations also provide for children a rich source of experience with real, personal, meaningful, two-way *language*. This language experience may be part of the foundation for reading skill. In fact, researchers interested in the development of literacy have begun to study the dinner-time conversations of young children for clues as to how early language paves the way to later reading ability (Beals & Snow, 1994). And one group of investigators has found that longer dinner times are associated with greater growth in reading skill from second to fifth grade (Anderson et al., 1988).

What might this have to do with television? There is not a lot of information to go on here, but it is interesting that Maccoby (1951) found in her very early study that about a third of TV families reported there was some tension over getting children to leave the TV and come to family meals. More than a fifth of the television-owning families dealt with the tension by frequently or always letting the children eat in front of the TV. These families succumbed to the attractions of television and, in so doing, traded some of the conversational give and take at mealtimes for one-way language from television. A more recent study of California sixth graders revealed that the television set was on during dinner in 59% of their homes (Medrich, Roizen, Rubin, & Buckley, 1982).

There is much we need to know before we can make definitive statements regarding television's influence on mealtime conversations and the possible long-term implications for reading. But of course we cannot forestall children's development until all the relevant information is available. In a sense, parents have to bet some portion of their children's reading ability on what enlightened common sense tells them to do about TV use at mealtimes.

Concluding Thoughts

We live in a time when reading ability seems to be in decline. Reading experience acquired during leisure hours offers a promising way to reverse the pattern of decline. Both family characteristics and hours devoted to the easy and pleasant activity of television watching are likely to influence children's leisure reading, which is typically viewed as more difficult than watching TV. In the context of home life, TV can be a very attractive alternative to reading and a potent distraction when one tries to read with the TV on. It may also be a deterrent to family mealtime conversations, themselves a potential contributor to reading ability. Young children who are just learning to read may be especially vulnerable to television's impact on reading.

Of course, almost all children with television in their homes do learn to read. The extent to which they might be better at reading or more broadly informed, had they grown up without TV, is an unanswered question.   We were able to obtain standardized reading or verbal achievement scores for only three of the no-TV children in our study. Their proficiency was very high (above the 97th percentile in all cases), but we do not know whether the other no-TV youngsters have attained or will ultimately attain similarly high reading achievement.   The fact that one child has a reading disorder—dyslexia—shows that growing up in a home without TV is not a guarantee of effortless reading achievement. With reading as with all other areas of children's development, parents have to make decisions based on limited information and on their own best judgment as to what is right for their particular family.

Chapter 7

Progeny and Profits

One thing I like [about not having television is that] it helps you be satisfied with a simpler way of life, because TV promotes materialism and it makes you dissatisfied with your circumstances. It makes you strive for a lot of things you don't necessarily need and it promotes the idea that half of [what you are] comes from owning.

— Barbara Field

I get terribly upset at the spiritual lack and the greed—things that are constantly as far as I can tell represented as desirable on TV—accumulation of goods, greed, and...lack of imagination.

— Eve Greenwald

The population is being manipulated by so many giant corporations.... I feel like our whole culture is getting to where you are being manipulated to do this and do that and do another thing.

— Ben Lott

[Television] necessarily aims at a market reduced to the lowest common denominator.

— Adam Lake

When you don't have television for a long time you become terribly intolerant of all those ads.... I can't look at the

television because I'm so bothered by the constant
interruption.

                                            – Adam Lake

I think...the commercials are especially bad.

                                        – Joellen Stelling

Mostly, what I'm offended with, with TV, is the ads.... The
shows you can kind of control. Turn the channel. But the
ads seem to all be the same. And I'm with Joellen,...to me
they're an insult to the intelligence.

                                          – Dave Stelling

The no-TV parents commonly state that they find the advertising
on TV to be offensive. They mention the implicit advocacy of materialist
values, the specter of corporate manipulation of television audiences, the
constant interruption of programming by advertisements, and lack of
viewer control over commercials.

The no-TV parents have not been alone in raising these concerns.
Experts from both journalistic and scientific disciplines have addressed
such issues and, in this chapter, we will take a look at what they have had
to say. Where relevant information is available, we will pay particular
attention to the influence of television advertising on children.

Before we move on, let's pause a moment to consider the basic
nature of the television business. Advertising is its heart and soul.
Television as we think of it would not exist without advertising. The
entertainment and information that come into our homes via commercial
channels are paid for by advertising. What advertisers get in return is
millions of eyes and ears trained on their commercial messages. As a TV
industry observer once put it, "In day-to-day commerce, television is not
so much interested in the business of communications as in the business
of delivering people to advertisers. People are the merchandise, not the
shows. The shows are merely bait" (Brown, 1971, pp. 15-16).

The implications of this simple fact about television are
enormous. In many ways, this chapter is about those implications. To
create a context for understanding them, let's look briefly at the history of
television advertising.

A Brief History of Television Advertising

The early development of the television industry in the United States was put on hold during World War II as the country focused its energies on winning the global conflict. But in October of 1945, amid nationwide post-war economic growth, the Federal Communications Commission (FCC) lifted bans that had been in effect during the war on issuing TV station licenses and on producing TV sets. The nascent television industry was then free to grow. During the remainder of the 1940s, television played second fiddle to radio. But by 1954, TV had already become the dominant medium for advertising in the U.S. (Matthei, 1997). Advertising dollars that had previously supported radio were diverted to the burgeoning television markets.

In those early days of television no one could be sure whether the new medium had a secure future or what its destiny was likely to be. As noted in the previous chapter, the families that waited the longest to buy a television set were often well-educated, professional families who felt uncertain about the ultimate value of television ownership (Maccoby, 1951).

It made economic sense, under the circumstances, to air programs that would appeal to those upscale families and thus stimulate them to purchase TV sets. So high-quality dramatic, musical, and children's programs appeared on television in abundance during the early 1950s (Brown, 1971). Children's programming was on TV daily, typically lasting into the early evening hours (Brown, 1977). Often it was aired as a public service, without commercial sponsorship (Condry, 1989). This programming strategy was apparently successful, as television had found its way into nearly all North American homes by 1960.

Television in the early days seemed to be surrounded by an aura of sophistication and refinement. The people who sold its advertising time were well-dressed, well-educated, cultured types who sold TV ads on the basis of their glamour appeal. It was very common for top broadcasting executives to have come up through the sales ranks of their organizations (Brown, 1971).

By the mid-1960s programming aimed at children faded in importance as advertisers turned their attentions toward adults, who had both money and power over how to spend it. Children's programs were no longer necessary to stimulate TV set purchases. They began to disappear from the daily TV roster and to be broadcast mainly on Saturday mornings, a time when the adult viewing audience was typically small anyway. A few early brush fires of protest about children's programming and advertising began to break out in the late 1960s and early 1970s, and government regulation of television was sometimes suggested as a way to solve perceived problems. As regulation became a concern, lawyers became increasingly important to broadcasters and, by the 1970s, top executives who had come up through the legal departments of broadcasting organizations occasionally joined the sales-oriented executives already at the top (Brown, 1971). The goal of both was maintenance and growth of industry profits in a competitive environment.

Against this historical backdrop, fine-tuning of the sponsorship and advertising picture was also taking place. In the earliest days of television, big corporate sponsors, with the help of ad agencies, commissioned independent producers to create shows that they would then sponsor. Entire shows were "brought to you" by a single sponsor, who had purchased an audience from a broadcaster (Matthei, 1997). In many ways, sponsors were identified with and linked to the programs they supported.

That arrangement began to change in the 1950s, when NBC pioneered an approach to advertising whereby the *network* produced and scheduled shows and advertisers bought time-slots within the shows in which to air their commercials. The new approach was labeled "participation" rather than "sponsorship." Now several parties collectively could pay for a single show. This opened up TV advertising to smaller companies who could not afford to sponsor and produce an entire program. When participation began, advertisers could purchase 60-second time-slots in which to air their commercials. In 1971, networks began selling 30-second slots (Matthei, 1997). Today even shorter time intervals are sold (Condry, 1989).

From the beginning, then, U.S. television has been a mixture of programs whose ostensible purpose is to *entertain* or *inform* viewers, and commercial messages, whose purpose is to *persuade* viewers—persuade them to buy something, or to like something, or to vote for something, or to do something. Theoretically, there is a distinction between shows and the many persuasive messages that accompany them. It has not gone unnoticed by advertisers, however, that the effectiveness of an ad is influenced both by the appeal of the ad itself and by the values of the program in which it appears (Thomas & Wolfe, 1995). This raises the question of how advertising affects programming.

How Ads Affect Programming

Advertisers understandably are willing to pay more to have an ad aired if it is likely to reach a very large audience than if it is going to reach only a small number of viewers. Accordingly, the most popular shows on television generate the biggest revenues for broadcasters. In other words, it is in broadcasters' interest to amass and deliver as large an audience as possible at each hour of the day and night. But not just any show appeals to a mass audience. Those that have been successful bait for huge audiences tend to offer escape from ordinary cares; they avoid unpleasant controversy and make the viewer tranquil enough that he or she will not stop watching (Brown, 1971; Kubey & Csikszentmihalyi, 1990). Comedies that do not stray too far into satire often serve these ends rather well. Depictions of violence apparently appeal to many viewers, perhaps because they hold audiences' attention and simultaneously enable them to feel safe from the "mean world" within the familiar fortress of the home. Sex, too, has obvious appeal as an attention-grabber. Interestingly, in their study of sexual content in prime-time shows, Sapolsky and Tabarlet (1991) found a perfect parallel between the amount of sex shown by a broadcast network and its programs' ratings (that is, its audience size). For two seasons, ten years apart, more sex was consistently accompanied by higher ratings.

The quest for the mass audience gathered momentum at the time when commercial sponsorship shifted from single corporate sponsors to participatory sponsorship. In the early days of television, corporations were occasionally willing to target smaller audiences in order to be identified with high-quality programs. But the situation changed when larger numbers of companies began shopping for commercial audiences. Audience size became the predominant concern. As this occurred, programming became less innovative and less experimental (Matthei, 1997). In fact it has been argued that industry personnel are under significant pressure to avoid programming failures and that this inevitably discourages innovation and encourages imitation on TV (Brown, 1971).

The situation that we have described was particularly true during the time when three networks accounted for virtually all of the television programming available to U.S. viewers. But television keeps changing and, as it does, the partitioning of the advertising dollar will change as well. The most notable development in recent years has been the adoption of cable and satellite TV by more and more households. In fact, in 1998 basic cable viewership outstripped broadcast network viewership for the first week ever in history (Shales, 1998). The mass audience is still much sought after and will remain so. Increasingly, though, cable channels are carving out niches for themselves among the country's television viewers.

Their advertising revenues will, of course, vary according to the size and composition of their audiences.

Once an audience is established—be it a mass audience or a smaller, specialized audience—advertisers will want to be assured of the composition of that audience and will want it to be as large as it possibly can be. A sporting goods manufacturer who sells to the youth market will continue to advertise on MTV only as long as MTV maintains its youth audience. This it must do by providing youth-oriented programming. The bait must be compatible with the pitch.

Advertising inevitably influences programming. The influence is indirect, but it is operative. If program producers are to be successful, they almost have to aim their productions at a particular advertising niche. Within limits, they can be creative. But the limits are determined by the audiences advertisers wish to reach and the state of mind they want viewers to be in when the commercials come on.

George Gerbner has pointed out that "the top 100 advertisers pay for two-thirds of all network television" (1996, p. xiii). That is to say that a huge proportion of the cultural products that come to us via television is being molded within limits set by a relatively small number of large corporations. Gerbner refers to these corporations as "our private 'Ministry of Culture'" (1996, p. xiii).

The downside of this situation is that small voices, complex topics, and unpopular or unsettling points of view tend not to appear very often on commercial television, be it broadcast or cable. This becomes a matter of poignant concern when we realize that TV is the major source of news and information for the majority of U.S. citizens (Comstock, 1989). But sometimes it is crucially important for society to hear the small voices and unpopular views. Sometimes it is necessary to deal with complexities. Our long-term survival as a culture may depend on our ability to challenge the status quo and think through difficult problems. It is very hard to accomplish such tasks on television with the TV business configured the way it is at the present time.

How TV Advertisements Work

The purpose of a commercial is to stimulate consumer interest in a product, often by anticipating consumers' uses for and gratifications from that product. Commercials are designed to get and hold viewers' attention so that the uses and gratifications can be depicted for them. Successful advertisements have to stand out—not only from the program but also from other ads. They are designed to coax viewers to remember and desire advertised products (Condry, 1989).

As you might imagine, there are many theories as to how commercials can be made as persuasive as possible. One such theory (Condry, 1989; McGuire, 1968) suggests that there are stages in the process of successful persuasion. These include:

- *exposure*: one must be exposed to the advertisement to be influenced by it;
- *attention*: the advertisement must be distinctive enough to garner attention;
- *comprehension*: the advertisement must be understood as the advertiser intends;
- *yielding*: the viewer must drop his or her defenses and believe the message;
- *retention*: the viewer must remember the advertised product at the time of purchase; and
- *deciding to buy*: the viewer must purchase the advertised product.

According to this theory, the successful producer of a commercial will have all of the stages of persuasion in mind as an advertisement is created. Another theory (Acuff, 1997) attaches additional stages to the process, including:

- *continuing to be satisfied with the product*; and
- *recommending the product to others.*

In short, there is much to be aware of and much to fit into a brief commercial message. Little wonder that the cost of producing a commercial is many times greater than the cost of producing programming, if one calculates costs per minute of air time (Condry, 1989). The commercials, not the programs, are the "big ticket" productions in an evening of television.

Linguistic analysis of the *verbal* content of advertisements has yielded some additional insights as to how advertisements work. Geis (1982) taped and analyzed some 800 commercials from news, prime-time, and children's programs. He discovered the following commonly-used verbal practices:

- shifting oral claims from weaker to stronger during the course of the ad;
- using illogical and misleading discourse;
- saying things that sound good but are meaningless;
- implying claims rather than stating them openly (such as saying a product tastes "fruity" when, in fact, it contains no fruit);

- presenting differing printed and verbal messages; and
- showing disclaimers in small print while drawing attention away from them with both sounds and pictures.

Under ordinary viewing conditions, of course, commercials go by rapidly without leaving time for audience members to study their content. Because of this, Geis believes, viewers are unlikely to see through the verbal obfuscation that may be employed. These techniques are understandable from the point of view of advertisers, who want to make the strongest case possible and still be able to defend it as true. However, ads may be misleading, even to adults. And children may be especially vulnerable to the zealous persuasiveness of a well-crafted commercial (Geis, 1982).

Children as a Target Audience

Children may be vulnerable, but that has not prevented them from being the target of advertising pitches. It is easy to understand why they would be. U.S. children under the age of 14 are estimated to spend $20 billion per year of their own money and to influence their parents' decisions in the expenditure of another $200 billion (Leonhardt & Kerwin, 1997). Manufacturers of products that appeal to children have an interest in collecting their share of these billions. A way to increase the likelihood that they will do so is to advertise to children.

Youngsters growing up in homes where television frequently accompanies family activities are immersed in advertising from infancy. Condry (1989) has estimated that the average child between 2 and 11 years of age is exposed to over 40,000 commercials per year. As youngsters start to watch children's programs on commercial stations— often by age 2 or 3—they begin to encounter significant numbers of ads for toys, breakfast cereals, snack foods, and fast foods. In recent times, advertisers of adult products and services—such as airlines, banks, hotels, automobiles, and computers—have also begun attempting to develop loyalties among child audiences (Leonhardt & Kerwin, 1997).

In the history of children's programming it has not been unusual for there to be 16 minutes of *nonprogram content* per TV hour. Nonprogram content includes product commercials, promotional messages regarding upcoming programs, and public service announcements (PSAs). Although there are occasionally straightforward announcements in nonprogram content, the bulk of it is persuasive in nature. Most of the persuasive messages are commercials (Condry, 1989). The actual number of minutes per hour devoted to advertising waxes and wanes as stations' economic status fluctuates.

For decades children's programming has carried more advertising per hour than adult prime-time programming. The reason for this is simple. Because the child audience is smaller, ads are cheaper and more of them must be sold to turn a profit. Another technique for making children's programming profitable has been to rerun programs up to six times over a two-year period. This practice saves program production costs and, at the same time, capitalizes on children's affinity for repetition (Comstock, 1991).

Children's programming on commercial television—the bait that lures them to the ads—typically attempts to appeal to as wide an age range as possible in order to maximize the size of the audience. Programs tailored to the specific cognitive and emotional needs of 3-year-olds, say, or 6-year-olds really are not economically feasible. Not only do they appeal to small audiences but they are also more costly to produce than the more familiar, noisy, high-action, animated offerings that are typically seen on commercial channels and that appeal to a broad 2- to 11-year-old audience.

Yes, children are an audience targeted by advertisers. But they have less money than adults and there aren't as many of them. The result is that children's programs on commercial television are heavily laced with advertising and are of lower quality than concerned parents might hope. Although children's programming on public television provides alternative, age-appropriate viewing options, research has shown that youngsters who start out watching educational programs often later "graduate" to commercial entertainment programming (Huston, Wright, Rice, Kerkman, & St. Peters, 1990).

What Children Understand

Given that children in TV households are likely to be exposed to thousands of commercials every year, it is reasonable to ask what sense they make of all that advertising. Researchers who have looked into this issue have been concerned with two general questions: (1) Do children recognize a commercial as different from a program? And (2) Do children understand that the intent of a commercial is to persuade them to buy something?

It turns out that the age of the child has a bearing on how these questions are answered. By age 4 or 5 children are able to distinguish commercials from regular programming. Not until the age of 8, however, do the majority of children understand that the intent of commercials is to sell. Children younger than 8 tend to believe that the ads are just trying to give them information (see Comstock, 1991; Condry, 1989; Kunkel, 2001; Liebert & Sprafkin, 1988). Also, those 5 to 10 years of age understand adult commercials somewhat less well than child commercials (Blosser & Roberts, 1985). As children get older and understand the purpose of ads more fully, they begin to distrust them. In spite of the distrust, the ads are still successful in influencing consumer behavior (Rossiter, 1979).

Children are initiated into the consumer culture little by little, with the aid of commercial television. That initiation apparently affects their real lives in numerous ways. Commercials have been shown to affect 5- to 8-year-olds' snack choices (Gorn & Goldberg, 1982). Observations of shoppers in the cereal aisles of Michigan grocery stores have revealed that children demand or request particular brands of cereal in 66% of cases in which parents and children shop together (Atkin, 1978). After being shown an adult ad for lipstick, young girls experience increased favorability toward the advertised brand (Gorn & Florsheim, 1985), suggesting that children are also affected by ads directed toward adults.

Children's understanding of commercials grows and changes as they get older. They need not understand fully in order to be swayed by commercial messages. Whether this is desirable from an ethical point of view is a question implicit in the no-TV parents' concerns about materialism.

Public Interest, Convenience, and Necessity

The Federal Communications Act of 1934 stipulated that, in order to be licensed to broadcast over public airwaves, a television station had to serve *"the public interest, convenience, and necessity."* This is a noble sounding phrase, but an ambiguous one. It was actually lifted out of earlier legislation that regulated the railroads and was written into the newer law to accomplish the dual purposes of stimulating the new and struggling TV business during the depths of the Great Depression and creating a basis for awarding broadcast licenses (Minow & LaMay, 1995).

The ambiguity of the public interest provision has allowed broadcasters to claim that they are serving the public interest so long as the public is interested in what they put on TV. This minimalist interpretation of the law has occasionally been challenged by child advocates, bureaucrats, and politicians, but generally it has been allowed to stand. There is understandable reluctance to dictate the content of programs or commercials in a country with constitutionally guaranteed freedom of speech.

Newton Minow is a former Chairman of the FCC and the author of the famous phrase describing television as a "vast wasteland," which he used in a speech in 1961. More recently he wrote, "In 1961, when I called television a 'vast wasteland,' I was thinking of an endless emptiness, a fallow field waiting to be cultivated and enriched. I never dreamed that we would fill it with toxic waste" (Minow, 1995). Minow and LaMay (1995) have argued that "the public interest" should be more than just a hollow phrase. They think that the public interest requirement dictates putting the interests of children ahead of the television industry's quest for profits. They believe this can be done constitutionally, while still protecting freedom of speech.

In the meantime, however, it is business as usual. Many children are likely to grow up and leave home before the public interest clause in the communications law grows its baby teeth—if, in fact, it ever does so. The no-TV parents are not waiting for that eventuality. They have taken matters into their own hands, without challenging the Constitution.

Concluding Thoughts

Commercial television is like a free advertising circular that is delivered to the home. It has enough tidbits of news and entertainment in it to get people to pick it up and look at it, but its real purpose is advertising. Television differs from the circular in that the ads are all read aloud, whether one is interested in them or not. You may not need a new car, but you are likely to see and hear entire automobile commercials. You may not be dissatisfied with your hair color, but you hear and see the hair-coloring ads anyway. If one mutes the ads one still sees their highly-produced visual images. Changing channels is largely ineffective, as advertising appears regularly on almost every channel.

An instructive exercise, we have found, is to videotape all the commercials and other nonprogram content from one hour of children's programming. This allows one to see, in 16 minutes or so, all the commercials and announcements a youngster would have seen in a fairly typical hour of television. Those who try this should not be surprised if they are troubled by what they see. The ads are often raucous and insistent and there are a great many of them.

Parents have to decide—actively or by default—how much commercial coaxing they want their children to be exposed to and how willing they are to tolerate the inevitable commercial "slant" in programming itself. The no-TV parents have eliminated the demanding presence of commercials, at least within their own homes.

Chapter 8

Summary and Discussion: Inner Resources

> We wanted our children to...develop self-sufficiency.
>
> – Barbara Field

> I wanted the children to be resourceful—not feeling like there always had to be something exciting going on before they could enjoy life.
>
> – Barbara Field

> But even apart from the question of reading, I believe not having television has allowed my children to develop the inner resources to amuse themselves in manifold ways.
>
> – Adam Lake

> I think these kids are better off.... I don't know how they'd be with a television, but I think...their ability to find things to do on their own is better.... In my opinion, you know, they're better than what they would have been had we had [TV].
>
> – Ben Lott

Implicit in the information given us by the no-TV parents is their belief that not having television to rely on will help their children develop "*inner resources*," to use the phrase of Adam Lake. These parents want their children to be self-reliant or, as Joellen Stelling put it, "to develop things on their own." Some of the parents stated this explicitly, as can be seen in the quotations above. But this is also a more general theme that seems to underlie their beliefs about child-rearing. We see it as a basic conviction—one that ties their other beliefs about raising children, and all four no-TV families, together.

In this chapter we will summarize the major points of earlier chapters and will also elaborate on the theme of developing inner resources. This will give us an opportunity to reconsider much of the information we have covered regarding television's roles in people's lives and to reflect upon that information in light of the issue of inner resources.

Defining "Inner Resources"

All of the parents who referred to the set of qualities we are focusing on here expressed their ideas in quite general terms. They spoke of their children's developing "self-sufficiency," being "resourceful," "amusing themselves," or finding "things to do on their own." We feel it is instructive to delineate some specific qualities that can be considered desirable inner resources. These are qualities that, by definition, reside *in* the individual; as such, they cannot be observed directly. The only way we can verify their existence is by seeing consistent evidence of them in an individual's overt behavior over a prolonged period of time. The intangible nature of such resources probably does not deter most parents —whether they have TV or not—from attempting to instill such qualities in their offspring.

Based on the statements of the no-TV parents, we define "inner resources" as *desirable internal qualities that strengthen an individual and enable him or her to create, independently and successfully, a meaningful life.* The specific characteristics that make up a given individual's arsenal of inner resources might include any or all of the following:

- *motivation or drive*: the energy to turn wishes into action;
- *autonomy*: self-direction;
- *a moral compass*: the character to pursue morally defensible aims;
- *knowledge about the world*: accurate information to buttress and guide one's actions;
- *self-knowledge*: a realistic view of one's own strengths and limitations;
- *the ability to see connections*: being able to discern important

relationships among various pieces of knowledge;
- *wisdom*: thinking clearly before acting and showing forbearance where appropriate;
- *self-confidence*: belief in one's own basic worth and ability;
- *courage*: the ability to maintain motivation in the face of fear; and
- *spirituality*: a sense of ultimate kinship with nature, the universe, or a god.

There may be characteristics that you would argue should be added to the list and we have no inherent quarrel with lengthening or revising it. However, we have attempted to limit it to qualities that the no-TV parents value in particular. It is most accurate to think of the list as a working approximation—against which it is possible to consider the various influences of television that we have been discussing in this book.

The summaries that follow cover Chapters 2 through 7, in which substantive findings regarding the effects of television were described. Each summary is then related to the topic of inner resources.

Time and Television

It is difficult to obtain an accurate measure of TV-watching time for people who live in homes with television, but conservative estimates place the average individual's viewing time at 2½ hours daily. This amounts to about 44% of an average person's leisure time (see Huston et al., 1992; Kubey & Csikszentmihalyi, 1990). Studies done in the early days of television showed that when TV first came to an area, people went to fewer movies, listened less to the radio, read less, and slept less. They also did somewhat less housework and out-of-home socializing, engaged in hobbies a bit less often, and attended church somewhat less frequently (see Comstock, 1991; Himmelweit, Oppenheim, & Vince, 1958; Schramm, Lyle, & Parker, 1961). Whether to interpret the changes as undesirable or as insignificant has been a matter of debate.

Data gathered more recently using the Experience Sampling Method (ESM) have shown adults watching TV during about 40% of their leisure time between 8:00 AM and 10:00 PM. More often than not (63.5% of the time) TV watching is shared with some other activity. People tend to give themselves low ratings on mood, activity level, and alertness when they are watching TV. Heavy viewers talk less, move around less, and leave home less than light viewers. Heavy viewers seem to be particularly uncomfortable when alone without any structured activity to engage in. They may turn to TV on such occasions and their heavy TV use may further diminish their ability to cope with unstructured free time (Kubey & Csikszentmihalyi, 1990).

Time and Inner Resources. It stands to reason that if people are to develop and refine their inner resources, they will need experience doing so. The general activity of creating a meaningful life on the strength of one's inner resources no doubt comes about as a result of creating numerous plans (not all of them successful), carrying out these plans, evaluating their results, and planning anew. Such painstaking experience in developing inner resources takes time.

It takes time to conjure up a plan—especially if one is a novice "planner," as young children inevitably are. It also generally takes time to carry out a plan. Further, numerous experiences with planning and following through are surely valuable—perhaps even necessary—in building the specific inner resources of motivation, self-confidence, knowledge about the world and the self, the ability to see connections, courage, wisdom, and a sense of autonomy. It seems reasonable to assert that building inner resources is a time-intensive undertaking. It is unlikely that it could be most successfully accomplished to the accompaniment of television—particularly if one considers that TV tends to lower mood, activity level, and alertness.

There is special reason to be concerned about heavy television viewers, who have greater than average difficulty acting autonomously in unstructured, solitary situations. Ironically, these people—who are probably most in need of experience acting on their own initiative—are least likely to get that experience because television is so frequently used to quell their discomfort. The case of the heavy viewers raises the possibility that some children may simply need more practice developing self-knowledge, self-confidence, and autonomy than others. Without anyone's intending for it to, TV may be particularly likely to hold such youngsters back.

The Content of Television

Violence on television has been monitored for many years. Violent behavior has always occurred frequently on TV, especially in programs designed for children, and it is not always presented so as to depict the pain and suffering that accompany it (see Cole, 1997; Huston & Wright, 1998; *National Television Violence Study*, 1997). A great deal of research has been done showing that exposure to televised violence is associated with increased aggressive behavior of various kinds in viewers (see Liebert & Sprafkin, 1988). Investigations using differing research approaches with differing age groups have yielded consistent results.

When televised violence is seen as "real" it is more likely to stimulate an aggressive response in the viewer than if it is seen as fantasy (Atkin, 1983; Berkowitz & Alioto, 1973; Jo & Berkowitz, 1994). This distinction loses its importance in children too young to tell the difference between reality and fantasy; such youngsters may interpret everything as "real." Studies have shown that children become desensitized to real-life violence after seeing televised aggression (Drabman & Thomas, 1976; Molitor & Hirsch, 1994). TV violence also helps to cultivate in viewers a belief that the world is a meaner and more dangerous place than it actually is (Bryant, Carveth, & Brown, 1981; Gerbner, Gross, Morgan, & Signorielli, 1994)

Sexual content on television has been increasing in the last two to three decades. Talking about sex remains the most usual type of sexual content, but more graphic depictions also occur. Sex between unmarried people is much more common than between married people on TV (see Buerkel-Rothfuss, 1993; Huston & Wright, 1998). It has been estimated that children who watch 9 hours of prime-time television per week see 1,400 sexual acts per year (Greenberg et al., 1993). Ethical considerations have prevented us from learning a great deal about how sex on TV influences youngsters.

Content and Inner Resources.
The fact that sex and violence occur so commonly on television may have implications for the development of children's inner resources. Most notably, heavy exposure to sexual and aggressive themes may create confusion in youngsters whose moral compasses are still being calibrated.

In many families, aggression as a way to solve interpersonal problems is frowned upon and actively discouraged. But even in families that are totally violence-free, television inevitably introduces the "aggressive alternative." We know from a great deal of research that televised violence sometimes has behavioral repercussions in children and we can hardly expect a child who has just hit a friend *not* trying to justify it to him- or herself. Once the self-justifying has begun, the aggression has become an *internal* experience for the child. This is not to say that the child will be morally "ruined" as a result, but that his or her beliefs about right and wrong may be more complicated and bewildering. Against a background of regular exposure to violence on television, moral judgments and justifications that would not be encouraged by the child's parents may result.

We have far less empirical evidence to go on in speculating about how sex on television influences the formation of children's inner resources. The worrisome possibility exists that youngsters who have seen a large number of televised sexual encounters (often without benefit of love) will feel empowered to act similarly when they themselves reach an age when such behavior seems appropriate. Even parents who have had the courage and knowledge to give their children good, sound information and advice about sex may be in competition with thousands of depictions of sexuality on TV. As is the case with aggression, moral confusion may be the result. We are suggesting, then, that the violent and sexual content of television, apart from the various other features of the medium, may be particularly likely to complicate the development of a very important inner resource—a moral compass.

The Question of Addiction

Survey data indicate that a majority of people believe that addiction to television is possible (see Kubey, 1996). Television addiction may begin with the phenomenon of attentional inertia whereby one's attention, if focused on the TV for 15 seconds or so, tends to remain there (see Anderson & Lorch, 1983).

Regarding longer-term involvement with television, some researchers have defined addiction simply as very heavy use of TV. Using this definition, some personality traits tend to be associated with heavy use. These include insecurity, rejection by peers, shyness, submissiveness, being easily bored, finding reality to be unpleasant, having a low sense of being in control, or feeling anxious when alone with nothing to do. TV may be very attractive to people with these characteristics. However, overuse of television may actually make these characteristics more pronounced (see Himmelweit et al., 1958; Kubey & Csikszentmihalyi, 1990; Schramm et al., 1961). Some heavy viewers may even meet the psychiatric criteria of the *DSM-IV* for a substance dependence disorder (Kubey, 1996).

Addiction and Inner Resources. By definition an addiction, or substance dependence disorder, involves investing one's time and energies in some external entity—a drug, say, or television. It is the very antithesis of developing inner resources. Youngsters with certain personality characteristics—such as being very shy, very submissive, or easily bored, for example—may be especially vulnerable to leaning so heavily on television that they fail to develop the inner resources needed to lead a truly self-directed life. Here again we see that those who most need experience developing their inner resources may be so drawn to television that they have little opportunity to learn skills that would enable them to entertain and direct themselves. A number of inner resources are apt to be casualties in a child who is addicted to TV. These would be likely to occur no matter what content the child typically prefers. Among the possible casualties we would include motivation, autonomy, knowledge about the world, self-knowledge, the ability to see connections, wisdom, self-confidence, courage, and spirituality.

Television and Thinking

Studying cognition—mental processes that must be inferred from behavior—is difficult and findings must be interpreted with caution. Attention span, or persistence, is a mental process that may be influenced by television-watching. High-action, violent shows seem to be particularly likely to shorten attention spans and make viewers less persistent (Anderson & Collins, 1988; Friedrich & Stein, 1973; MacBeth, 1996).

Because television is primarily an entertainment medium, viewers tend to develop a belief that TV is "easy." Consequently, they invest less mental effort in television-watching than in many other activities (see Kerkman, Piñon, Wright, & Huston, 1996). ESM data show that levels of concentration while watching TV are low (Kubey & Csikszentmihalyi, 1990). The limited information that is available suggests, as well, that television is detrimental to young children's creativity (see MacBeth, 1996; Singer, 1993; van der Voort & Valkenburg, 1994). And there is additional evidence of an adverse effect on creative problem-solving in older children and adults (Suedfeld et al., 1986).

The formal features commonly used in children's shows are attractive to viewers but probably interfere with reflective thought during viewing (Huston et al., 1981; Singer & Singer, 1983). Television has been described as a medium of "missing information" in that its subject matter is inherently limited to what is easily televisable and appealing to a large audience (McKibben, 1992).

Thinking and Inner Resources. Thinking is really a feature of all the items on our list of inner resources. The ability to think—creatively and logically—may be particularly valuable in reasoning about moral issues, evaluating knowledge about the world and oneself, seeing connections, exercising wisdom, and perhaps developing spirituality as well. In all of these inner activities, one must generate a set of ideas and make selections among them on some basis. The type of thinking required in all cases is likely to take time and effort. Given television's apparent effects on thinking, it is probable that thinking skills will flourish best during times when children are not watching TV.

We are reminded here of Barbara Field's fondness for silence, for it may be in periods of silence that people are most attuned to their thoughts. They may hear them most clearly and judge them most accurately when there are the fewest outside distractions. At the very least, being attuned to one's own thoughts, in the absence of the intrusions of television, would surely be unlikely to *interfere* with developing one's inner resources.

Reading and Watching

Reading skills seem to have been in decline in the U.S. since the 1970s (Beentjes & van der Voort, 1988; Glenn, 1994). Early studies showed that some decreases in reading were associated with the introduction of television. Children who are just learning to read may be especially vulnerable to displacement of reading time (see Corteen & Williams, 1986).

Correlational studies have shown a complex relationship between television viewing and reading achievement. For elementary and middle school children, there appears to be a curvilinear relationship such that a little TV viewing is associated with somewhat better reading achievement than no viewing at all, but very high levels of viewing are associated with very low reading scores (see Neuman, 1988). Such findings are difficult to interpret, because the children who do not watch any TV may be non-watchers for a variety of different reasons. For high school students, reading scores tend to drop in a straightforward, linear manner as viewing time increases (Neuman, 1988).

Television may be a deterrent to reading because watching it is easy, whereas reading can be difficult. Children—especially those needing extra practice in reading—may tend to avoid reading and gravitate instead to television (see Comstock, 1991; Corteen & Williams,

1986). Trying to read and watch TV at the same time poses a problem because research has shown that a television playing in the background disrupts reading comprehension (Armstrong & Greenberg, 1990).

Reading ability may be forged in part out of experiences with conversational language. If TV inhibits conversation—perhaps by being on during family meals—it could have an additional, indirect effect on reading (see Anderson, Wilson, & Fielding, 1988; Beals & Snow, 1994; Maccoby, 1951).

Reading and Inner Resources. Children who are excellent readers have open to them a huge range of information sources. They can quite readily gain access to a far broader and more detailed set of information than would be available to them via television. On the list of inner resources, it is arguable that reading is especially suited to gaining knowledge about the world. A child who reads well and has a solid and expanding store of knowledge will doubtless benefit as well by being able to see additional and more complex connections among facts. These strengths may in turn enhance motivation, autonomy, wisdom, self-confidence, and courage. Learning to read well is a no-lose proposition. It is best accomplished with the television off, especially for youngsters with particular reading difficulties.

Progeny and Profits

TV programming is supported by advertisers, who pay for programming designed to lure audiences to their commercial messages. In the early days of television, high quality programming was used to entice upscale families to purchase television sets. Once nearly all households had TV, the mass audience became the preoccupation of broadcasters who understandably wished to sell advertising time for the highest possible price (Brown, 1971).

Advertisements influence programming because advertisers want to reach a mass audience in a receptive mood. Only programming that provides this will be consistently supported by advertisers. Light comedy, violence, and sex often draw large audiences (Brown, 1971; Matthei, 1997).

Commercials are attention-getting and are carefully designed to *persuade* viewers to drop defenses and buy advertised products and services. They cost much more to produce than programs, per unit of air time. Advertisements may mislead the viewer, particularly if the viewer is a child (see Condry, 1989; Geis, 1982).

Children influence the spending of an estimated $220 billion per year and are therefore an attractive target for advertisers (Leonhardt & Kerwin, 1997). To make children's programming profitable, however, more ads must be sold than is the case for prime-time programming. Also, the programs must appeal to a broad age-range in order to maximize the size of the child audience (see Comstock, 1991; Condry, 1989). Children recognize commercials as different from programs by age 4 or 5, but they typically do not understand the persuasive intent of advertisements until age 8 or so (see Comstock, 1991; Condry, 1989; Liebert & Sprafkin, 1988). Even if they are not fully understood, commercials affect children's choices of advertised products (Blosser & Roberts, 1985).

Profits and Inner Resources. Commercial television is a marketplace, a midway in which corporations display and extol their wares. Any inner resources developed there are likely to have a decidedly materialistic slant. Some families will undoubtedly see nothing wrong with this and may think of it as healthy. Others may find themselves in a chronic struggle with advertisers over the inner resources of their children. The degree of struggle is likely to depend on how much a particular family tolerates or rejects materialistic values.

Our no-TV parents would probably agree that the inner qualities of autonomy and spirituality are greatly at odds with the persuasive, profit-driven nature of television. Autonomy or self-direction carries with it the connotation of not falling prey to persuasion by others, particularly when their motive is their own profit. And spirituality—focusing on the spirit rather than the body—is inherently nonmaterialistic. We would argue, too, that the ability to see connections is likely to be jeopardized by television's fundamentally persuasive core. Its simplistic portrayal of connections, both within commercial messages and within the programs that lure viewers to the commercials, may very well detract from children's abilities to draw their own connections. It is further possible that if autonomy, spirituality, and the ability to see connections have been adversely affected, wisdom and the individual's moral compass may fail to thrive as well.

Concluding Thoughts

Earlier, we defined inner resources as desirable internal qualities that strengthen an individual and enable him or her to create, independently and successfully, a meaningful life. On the list of such resources we included motivation, autonomy, a moral compass, knowledge about the world, self-knowledge, the ability to see connections, wisdom, self-confidence, courage, and spirituality. It is doubtful whether one could find many parents anywhere who would disagree with these as worthwhile qualities to instill in their children. A great many, however, have probably thought very little about the implications of family television use for the development of these qualities. Some of them will perhaps be grateful that our no-TV parents *have* thought about these issues.

In each of our interviews with the no-TV families, we asked what they thought were the most important problems facing society today. The major themes that arose in their replies were *overpopulation*, *materialism and greed*, and *lack of spirituality*. It is interesting that they selected these particular issues as especially noteworthy. All the issues can be related directly or indirectly to items on our list of inner resources. Overpopulation may be influenced by people's lack of knowledge about the world, inability to see connections, lapses in wisdom, and perhaps failures of courage as well. Materialism and greed may result from moral confusion, deficiencies in knowledge, or a lack of self-confidence. The spirituality issue is already on the list. We believe it is not going beyond the no-TV families' intended meaning to suggest that they feel the major problem in society is widespread *failure of people to develop adequate inner resources*. It may be easier to discern this after living a few years without television.

Chapter 9

Drawbacks and Benefits of Living Without Television

We've found that most adults get extremely defensive.
> – Eve Greenwald

A...common response that I've observed is that people will get real defensive when you tell them. The most common responses...I get are they say, "Oh, well, we really only watch the news," or "We only watch public television," or "We don't even have cable." As if...my not having a TV is somehow indicting them, which it's not.
> – Laura Lott

The biggest defense of people is, "Well, we only watch sports," "Well, we only watch Discovery channel," "Well, we only watch the History channel," "We only watch the Learning channel."
> – Joellen Stelling

We've found our family was most defensive about it.... We have a brother-in-law that won't really come over to our house because we don't have a TV.... My father is...not mean but a little sarcastic about us not having a TV.
> – Joellen Stelling

When I was working at ____, ...there were a couple [of
people] there that kind of, almost ridiculed me for the idea of
not having a set.

– Nelson Field

Children teased [both my children] for being poor.... You
know, like "Can't even afford a TV."

– Adam Lake

Yeah...[the children] still lobby [for TV]. Even after thirteen
years, they still lobby on a regular basis to have one.

– Laura Lott

It's not the easiest thing on earth not to have a TV. I mean,
it would be so easy when they're under your feet, just, "Here,
go watch this," or "Go pop a movie," or "Just go watch
anything. Get away from me for a half an hour."

– Dave Stelling

We might well have had plenty more quiet evenings and a
few nicer evenings with friends if we had a den where all the
children could be parked in front of the tube.

– Eve Greenwald

If you go for years [without television]...you don't know who
anybody is... *People* magazine...is a sea of meaningless
names.

– Adam Lake

It was like about a month to six weeks where you really kind
of [feel] something's missing. And then you kind of get over
it.

– Dave Stelling

We will not have a TV. At least not for a long time. Until
[the children] are well developed.

– Dave Stelling

I think it would be a lot harder...[to get rid of the TV] if we
ever had one.

– Laura Lott

Everyone who finds out says, "Oh boy, I wish I could do

that." I think, "Well, just try it for a month; just unplug the thing." I [think] that it [is] quite interesting that people can't just back away from it.... It would be interesting to see what would happen if more people would just go for a walk, or read together, or just go plant some flowers.

– Dave Stelling

Watching TV is not a "together" thing.

– Joellen Stelling

Living without television is not a cure for all of life's problems. It may improve matters in some ways and at the same time create new difficulties of its own. Each family that considers living without TV must evaluate the decision in light of its own particular composition, habits, and needs. Family members will need to weigh and balance the potential benefits and drawbacks for their household. Although our no-TV families —especially the parents—give living without television a glowing report, they also are candid about drawbacks. Here, we will describe the drawbacks they have encountered and then move on to consider the words of encouragement they offer.

Drawbacks

As reflected in the quotes at the beginning of this chapter, the drawback mentioned most often by the no-TV families is negative reactions by other people. The parents are usually the ones to draw criticism, but the Greenwald-Lake children have been teased as well. The two older Lott children do not say they've been teased, but do report that their friends ask why they do not have TV. Friends of the Field youngsters have always known that the family does not have a TV and do not raise the issue. The Stelling children are too young to have faced peer judgments yet.

No-TV parents have often encountered what they perceive to be defensiveness in TV-owning acquaintances. Upon hearing of a family's not having TV, people are often quick to justify their own television use. In some cases they may be saying "I only watch the news" or "I only watch educational television" as a way of agreeing with the no-TV parents that much of the programming on television is not very worthwhile. But psychological defensiveness may also frequently underlie such comments. In fact, research in the U.S., Britain, and Japan has shown that people quite commonly feel guilty about watching television, especially if they watch a great deal (see Kubey & Csikszentmihalyi, 1990). People's quickness to justify their own television use—often in circumstances where there is no necessity for them to mention it at all—may bespeak a subtle feeling of guilt on their part. Whatever the case, parents who decide to live without television should be aware that some family members, friends, and acquaintances will react negatively to their decision. The no-TV parents all told us that they have learned to avoid the matter most of the time simply by not bringing up the issue of television.

The Lotts report that some of their children regularly ask for their parents to get a TV and the Stellings say that their son and daughter frequently beg to go next door and watch the neighbor's television. (Interestingly, they have not yet asked to have a TV in their own home.) The Field and Greenwald-Lake children are content with not having TV. So children differ in how readily they take to a no-TV decision, even in families that have always been without television. Parents considering doing away with their own TVs will have to balance potential benefits against the likely reactions of their children. In this regard it is worth considering Laura Lott's observation that it would be harder to get rid of the TV after one's children had already become accustomed to watching it.

Two no-TV parents—Eve Greenwald and Dave Stelling—told us that they know television might ease some of the demands of parenting if it were available. They recognize, as most parents do, the attractiveness of TV as a live-in babysitter. It is interesting in this regard that Maccoby, in her 1951 study of early TV owners, found that 54% of the mothers she interviewed said TV made it easier for them to take care of their children. One mother likened it to putting her children to sleep. Others appreciated that the TV kept the children inside where adults could be assured of their safety. Parents choosing the no-TV option have to be willing to forfeit the babysitting function along with the television itself.

Adam Lake speaks about the type of information one has access to without television and points out that he receives plenty of information on current events, politics, and many other topics. But one area he does not know about is television itself. TV celebrities who are known to millions are often not known to him. Of course, the longer one lives without television the more this is likely to be the case. So people eyeing the no-TV lifestyle need to be aware that if they want information on TV culture they will have to seek it in alternative ways.

Contemporary families who have *long-term* experience without television are such a rarity that they have not really appeared in the scientific literature. There have been a very few studies on short-term television deprivation, however. The results of some of these studies raise a suspicion of TV addiction. Tan (1977) recruited 17 married couples (and their children), 9 single women, and 8 single men all of whom agreed to leave their TVs off for 6 days in August of 1974. Tan was unable to get a random sample because so few families originally contacted would agree to participate. This researcher ended up with a highly educated group, 55% of whom were college graduates and 24% of whom were graduate students. After 6 days, 34% reported they had missed TV "very much" or "quite a bit" (Tan, 1977, p. 377). Another study of short-term TV deprivation was conducted in Sweden. There, a 17-day television strike in 1980 afforded investigators an opportunity to assess the reactions of 17-year-olds. Few of the teenagers studied reported feeling strongly deprived (Windahl, Höjerback, & Hedinsson, 1986).

Winick (1988) used the ingenious approach of interviewing New York City families whose TV sets were being repaired or had been stolen. He interviewed 680 families between 1976 and 1982. (All homes had had just one TV set.) His subjects typically felt worst during the first 3 or 4 days and reported anxiety, aggression, boredom, irritation and disruptions in their routines; 80% experienced a moderate to severe reaction. By the second week most began to adapt to not having TV. Heavy viewers missed television the most. Those with more education and more ties outside the home adapted better than others. About a fourth of the families had a reaction "akin to the reaction...after the death of a beloved person or...[after becoming] unemployed" (Winick, 1988, p. 222). Husband-wife relationships that had been good remained so, but those that had been problematic seemed to get worse. Children sometimes began to be more of a bother to their parents. Some people complained of not being able to get away from the rest of the family. The vast majority (98%) planned to replace the missing TV.

Scientific accounts, then, warn of the possibility of a strongly negative immediate reaction to removing television. Not surprisingly, this is likely to be more pronounced in heavy viewers. In particular, some of the reactions described by Winick's families with broken or stolen TV sets sound a lot like addictive behavior. What this means for people contemplating life without television is that the first few days and weeks are likely to be quite difficult, especially if there are TV-dependent people in the family.

Journalistic evidence, too, suggests that removing the television can have some attendant difficulties. Winn (1985) noted that parents temporarily without TV missed being able to discipline their children by removing television privileges. And families who lived for many years without television reported having difficulty getting babysitters. Dullea (1974) found that some no-TV parents were dismayed when children were given homework assignments based on TV. (The babysitter and homework issues were brought up briefly by one of our no-TV families.) Daley (1978), a father of three, recounted what happened when he disabled the family television set. The first week was "sheer hell" (Daley, 1978, p. 144), but by the fourth week the children had found other things to do and no longer mentioned the TV.

Before we leave the topic of drawbacks, let's reconsider an idea that has appeared often enough in this book to warrant being called a theme. It is that heavy viewers—TV-dependent individuals—are often the very people most in need of a break from television. They probably have skills and capacities—inner resources—that they badly need to work on. Unfortunately, it is likely that it will be hardest for these viewers to give up (or cut back on) television. Further, they will not be likely to benefit a great deal unless new, healthier activities replace watching TV. Their families will have to plan carefully and show a lot of patience if they hope to make the switch successfully.

Benefits

Several things can be said by way of encouragement for families who want to try the no-TV option. First, we note that our no-TV parents —some of whom are professed TV addicts themselves—are very happy with their decision not to have TV. Seven of the eight rated themselves as "extremely satisfied" with not having TV—the highest possible rating on a 7-point scale. The eighth rated her satisfaction as a 6—the next-highest rating. Of the eight children who expressed a personal opinion about it, only one was frankly dissatisfied. One appeared to be "on the fence" and the other six were by and large content to live without television.

Probably one of the reasons these families have adjusted so well to life without television is that it is all their children have ever known. None of these youngsters became reliant on TV and then had to adapt to its removal. Given the extreme short-term reactions people often have to the loss of television, making the decision before the children arrive surely promises to be the most painless way to proceed. But even doing that will require the adults to adjust. Those wanting to do so may be encouraged by Dave Stelling's observation that it only took a month to 6 weeks to get used to not having a TV.

Families considering the no-TV option should also realize that they can change their minds later. If being without television does not accomplish what they hope it will or if it creates unexpected problems, it is an easy decision to undo. An even more likely eventuality, we suspect, is that the children will reach an age when television in the home no longer poses quite the same threat it might have when they were younger. Once youngsters' inner resources, interests, and abilities are strongly developed, television probably will not have the appeal it would have had earlier. Dave Stelling expresses this when he says that his family will not have TV until the children are "well developed." In fact, some investigators have gathered evidence showing that children who read more have better understanding of television science programs (Clifford, Gunter, & McAleer, 1995). If reading enhances learning from television, it makes sense to first become proficient at reading and to take up television later.

Another encouraging feature of the no-TV option is how very simple it is. Once the television is gone there is no immediate temptation. There is no need to debate the details of television use. Members of the family can just go about the business of adjusting. Children may raise the issue of acquiring TV, but that is likely to be the sole point of contention. The early days of "sheer hell" may still happen, but there is no way to renege because the TV is not there. It is possible that it would be easier for parents to enforce a total ban when television is absent from the home than to enforce a cut-back when the TV is present, especially if they are busy and their children are old enough to argue.

Finally, the greatest encouragement for raising children without television is the expectation of the ways in which they will benefit. Based on the experiences of the four no-TV families and the research we have covered, future no-TV families have reason to expect more conversation, more reading, better reading achievement, clearer thinking, less aggression, a more quiet and peaceful home environment, and more strongly developed inner resources in their children. Our no-TV youngsters are testimony to the fact that this can be done without creating cultural or social misfits.

But Wait...

We want to make it clear that we are not advocating the no-TV life here. Rather, we have been examining it. If it looks like an attractive option, it is because the no-TV families have carried it off so well and because there is substantial support for many of their views in the scientific literature. Notice that in all four of our no-TV families the two spouses were in agreement with one another about the decision not to have television. We suspect that this is an important reason for the satisfaction they have experienced.

Whether or not to have television is a decision that families can only make for themselves. Those who consider it should think about it carefully and avoid feeling pressured. It is a decision that will work only if it fits the individuals involved.

Concluding Thoughts

Parents who are concerned about the issues raised in this book have many options open to them. They may restrict their children's viewing time or the program content they allow their youngsters to see. They may disallow television during the school week but permit children to watch recorded programs on weekends (see MacBeth, 1996). They may rely on V-chip technology in conjunction with industry ratings of program content. They may use some combination of these options. Whether these parents succeed or fail in their attempts to control TV use will depend in some measure on the ages and inclinations of their children. In many cases, they may find themselves embroiled in ongoing negotiations regarding television use.

Those who choose not to have television in their homes will avoid the rule-making and negotiating likely to accompany other options. They will, however, risk lobbying by their children and will join a virtually invisible minority in our society. No-TV families have been largely ignored or slighted by scientists; we found several references where, in passing, they were dismissed as ignorant, unimportant, or misguided. Horkheimer (1974) said that removing TV was equivalent to fleeing into the past and would result in maladjustment in children. Miller (1988) said that living without TV consigns one to "a life of touristic ignorance" (p. 10) about one's culture. Others suggested that only "a few teachers and moralists" (Barwise & Ehrenberg, 1988, p. 138) disapprove of television. Beentjes and van der Voort (1988) felt the scientific study of TV-lessness is virtually impossible because of its rarity.

It is interesting that these are all references from the 1970s and 1980s. We anticipate that the no-TV minority may start to grow in numbers and become a bit more visible—to both the scientific community and the person on the street. One reason we think so is that television is getting worse. There has been an increase in overall time devoted to non-program content during prime-time (at an all-time high of almost 16 minutes per hour in 1998); air time is cluttered with more, shorter ads; and competitive pressures are prompting an ever-more-frantic bid for the mass audience (Moore, 1999; "Study finds," 1998). If these trends continue, more families may opt out of television, at least while their children are young.

References

Abramson, P. R. (1992). *A case for case studies: An immigrant's journal.* Newbury Park, CA: Sage.

Acuff, D. S. (With Reiher, R. H.). (1997). *What kids buy and why: The psychology of marketing to kids.* New York: The Free Press.

American Psychiatric Association. (1994). *Diagnostic and statistical manual of mental disorders* (4th ed). Washington, DC: Author.

Anderson, D. R., Alwitt, L. F., Lorch, E. P., & Levin, S. R. (1979). Watching children watch television. In G. A. Hale & M. Lewis (Eds.), *Attention and cognitive development* (pp. 331-361). New York: Plenum.

Anderson, D. R., & Collins, P. A. (1988). *The impact on children's education: Television's influence on cognitive development.* Washington, DC: U.S. Department of Education.

Anderson, D. R., Levin, S. R., & Lorch, E. P. (1977). The effects of TV program pacing on the behavior of preschool children. *AV Communication Review, 25,* 154-166.

Anderson, D. R., & Lorch, E. P. (1983). Looking at television: Action or reaction? In J. Bryant & D. R. Anderson (Eds.), *Children's understanding of television: Research on attention and comprehension* (pp. 1-33). New York: Academic Press.

Anderson, D. R., Lorch, E. P., Field, D. E., Collins, P. A., & Nathan, J. G. (1986). Television viewing at home: Age trends in visual attention and time with TV. *Child Development, 57,* 1024-1033.

Anderson, R. C., Wilson, P. T., & Fielding, L. G. (1988). Growth in reading and how children spend their time outside of school. *Reading Research Quarterly, 13,* 285-303.

Armstrong, G. B., & Greenberg, B. S. (1990). Background television as an inhibitor of cognitive processing. *Human Communication Research, 16,* 355-386.

Armstrong, G. B., & Sopory, P. (1997). Effects of background television on phonological and visuo-spatial working memory. *Communication Research, 24,* 459-480.

Atkin, C. (1983). Effects of realistic TV violence vs. fictional violence on aggression. *Journalism Quarterly, 60*(4), 615-621.

Atkin, C. K. (1978). Observation of parent-child interaction in supermarket decision-making. *Journal of Marketing, 42,* 41-45.

Bandura, A. (1965). Influence of models' reinforcement contingencies on the acquisition of imitative responses. *Journal of Personality and Social Psychology, 1,* 589-595.

Bandura, A., Ross, D., & Ross, S. A. (1961). Transmission of aggression through imitation of aggressive models. *Journal of Abnormal and Social Psychology, 63,* 575-582.

Bandura, A., Ross, D., & Ross, S. A. (1963). Imitation of film-mediated aggressive models. *Journal of Abnormal and Social Psychology, 66,* 3-11.

Barwise, P., & Ehrenberg, A. (1988). *Television and its audience.* Newbury Park, CA: Sage.

Beals, D. E., & Snow, C. E. (1994). "Thunder is when the angels are upstairs bowling": Narratives and explanations at the dinner table. *Journal of Narrative and Life History, 4,* 331-352.

Bechtel, R. B., Achelpohl, C., & Akers, R. (1972). Correlates between observed behavior and questionnaire responses on television viewing. In E. A. Rubinstein, G. A. Comstock, & J. P. Murray (Eds.), *Television and social behavior: Vol. 4. Television in day-to-day life: Patterns of use* (pp. 274-344). Washington, DC: U.S. Government Printing Office.

Beentjes, J. W. J., & van der Voort, T. H. A. (1988). Television's impact on children's reading skills: A review of research. *Reading Research Quarterly, 23,* 389-413.

Berkowitz, L., & Alioto, J. T. (1973). The meaning of an observed event as a determinant of its aggressive consequences. *Journal of Personality and Social Psychology, 28,* 206-217.

Bernard, A. (1990, March). Just say no. *Savvy Woman, 11,* 88, 87.

Blosser, B. J., & Roberts, D. F. (1985). Age differences in children's perceptions of message intent: Responses to TV news, commercials, educational spots, and public service advertisements. *Communication Research, 12*(4), 455-484.

Brown, J. D., White, A. B., & Nikopoulou, L. (1993). Disinterest, intrigue, resistance: Early adolescent girls' use of sexual media content. In B. S. Greenberg, J. D. Brown, & N. L. Buerkel-Rothfuss (Eds.), *Media, sex, and the adolescent* (pp. 177-195). Cresskill, NJ: Hampton.

Brown, J. R., Cramond, J. K., & Wilde, R. J. (1974). Displacement effects of television and the child's functional orientation to media. In J. G. Blumler & E. Katz (Eds.), *The uses of mass communications: Current perspectives on gratifications research* (pp. 93-112). Thousand Oaks, CA: Sage.

Brown, L. (1971). *Televi$ion: The business behind the box.* New York: Harcourt Brace Jovanovich.

Brown, L. (1977). *The New York Times encyclopedia of television.* New York: Times Books.

Bryant, J., Carveth, R. A., & Brown, D. (1981). Television viewing and anxiety: An experimental examination. *Journal of Communication, 31,* 106-119.

Buerkel-Rothfuss, N. L. (1993). Background: What prior research shows. In B. S. Greenberg, J. D. Brown, & N. L. Buerkel-Rothfuss (Eds.), *Media, sex, and the adolescent* (pp. 5-18). Cresskill, NJ: Hampton.

Bushman, B. J., & Huesmann, L. R. (2001). Effects of televised violence on aggression. In D. G. Singer & J. L. Singer (Eds.), *Handbook of children and the media* (pp. 223-254). Thousand Oaks, CA: Sage.

California Assessment Program. (1982). *Survey of sixth grade school achievement and television viewing habits.* Sacramento, CA: California State Department of Education.

Clifford, B. R., Gunter, B., & McAleer, J. (1995). *Television and children: Program evaluation, comprehension, and impact.* Hillsdale, NJ: Erlbaum.

Cole, J. (1997). *The UCLA television violence report, 1997.* Los Angeles: UCLA Center for Communication Policy.

Comstock, G. (1989). *The evolution of American television.* Newbury Park, CA: Sage.

Comstock, G. (With Paik, H.). (1991). *Television and the American child.* San Diego, CA: Academic Press.

Condry, J. (1989). *The psychology of television.* Hillsdale, NJ: Erlbaum.

Corteen, R. S., & Williams, T. M. (1986). Television and reading skill. In T. M. Williams (Ed.), *The impact of television: A natural experiment in three communities* (pp. 39-86). Orlando, FL: Academic Press.

Creswell, J. W. (1994). *Research design: Qualitative and quantitative approaches.* Thousand Oaks, CA: Sage.

Daley, E. A. (1978). *Father feelings.* New York: Morrow.

Desmond, R. (2001). Free reading. In D. G. Singer & J. L. Singer (Eds.), *Handbook of children and the media* (pp. 29-45). Thousand Oaks, CA: Sage.

Diamond, D. (1996, January). Life without TV: How one family conquered its tube addiction. *Parents Magazine, 71*(1), 87-88.

Donnerstein, E., & Smith, S. (2001). Sex in the media: Theory, influences, and solutions. In D. G. Singer & J. L. Singer, (Eds.), *Handbook of children and the media* (pp. 289-307). Thousand Oaks, CA: Sage.

Drabman, R. S., & Thomas, M. H. (1976). Does watching violence on television cause apathy? *Pediatrics, 57,* 329-331.

Dullea, G. (1974, December 20). No TV in the house--and they want it that way. *The New York Times,* p. 44.

Dunn, J. (1996). Family conversations and the development of social understanding. In B. Bernstein & J. Brannen (Eds.), *Children, research and policy* (pp. 81-95). London: Taylor & Francis.

Finkel, D. (1994, January 16). TV without guilt, group portrait with television: One family's love affair with the tube. *The Washington Post Magazine,* 9-15, 24-27.

Friedrich, L. K., & Stein, A. H. (1973). Aggressive and prosocial television programs and the natural behavior of preschool children. *Monographs of the Society for Research in Child Development, 38* (4, Serial No. 151).

Geis, M. L. (1982). *The language of television advertising.* New York: Academic Press.

Gerbner, G. (1996). Forward: Invasion of the storytellers. In R. F. Fox, *Harvesting minds: How TV commercials control kids* (pp. ix-xiii). Westport, CT: Praeger.

Gerbner, G., Gross, L., Morgan, M., & Signorielli, N. (1994). Growing up with television: The cultivation perspective. In J. Bryant & D. Zillmann (Eds.), *Media effects: Advances in theory and research* (pp. 17-41). Hillsdale, NJ: Erlbaum.

Gerbner, G., Gross, L., Signorielli, N., Morgan, M., & Jackson-Beeck, M. (1979). The demonstration of power: Violence Profile No. 10. *Journal of Communication, 29,* 177-196.

Glenn, N. (1994). Television watching, newspaper reading, and cohort differences in verbal ability. *Sociology of Education, 67,* 216-230.

Gorn, G. J., & Florsheim, R. (1985). The effects of commercials for adult products on children. *Journal of Consumer Research, 11,* 962-967.

Gorn, G. J., & Goldberg, M. E. (1982). Behavioral evidence of the effects of televised food messages on children. *Journal of Consumer Research, 9,* 200-205.

Greenberg, B. S., Stanley, C., Siemicki, M., Heeter, C., Soderman, A., & Linsangan, R. (1993). Sex content on soaps and prime-time television series most viewed by adolescents. In B. S. Greenberg, J. D. Brown, & N. L. Buerkel-Rothfuss (Eds.), *Media, sex, and the adolescent* (pp. 29-44). Cresskill, NJ: Hampton.

Greenfield, P. M., Yut, E., Chung, M., Land, D., Kreider, H., Pantoja, M., & Horsley, K. (1993). The program-length commercial: A study of the effects of television/toy tie-ins on imaginative play. In G. L. Berry & J. K. Asamen (Eds.), *Children and television: Images in a changing sociocultural world* (pp. 53-72). Newbury Park, CA: Sage.

Hafner, A., Ingels, S., Schneider, B., & Stevenson, D. (1990). *National Education Longitudinal Study of 1988: A profile of the American eighth grader: NELS:88 Student descriptive summary.* Washington, DC: U.S. Government Printing Office.

Harrison, L. F., & Williams, T. M. (1986). Television and cognitive development. In T. M. Williams (Ed.), *The impact of television: A natural experiment in three communities* (pp. 87-142). Orlando, FL: Academic Press.

Hearold, S. (1986). A synthesis of 1043 effects of television on social behavior. In G. Comstock (Ed.), *Public communication and behavior, Vol. 1* (pp. 65-133). Orlando, FL: Academic Press.

Himmelweit, H. T., Oppenheim, A. N., & Vince, P. (1958). *Television and the child: An empirical study of the effect of television on the young.* London: Oxford University Press.

Horkheimer, M. (1974). *Critique of instrumental reason.* New York: Seabury.

Hornik, R. (1978). Television access and the slowing of cognitive growth. *American Educational Research Journal, 15,* 1-15.

Huesmann, L. R. (1986). Psychological processes promoting the relation between exposure to media violence and aggressive behavior by the viewer. *Journal of Social Issues, 42,* 125-139.

Huesmann, L. R., Eron, L. D., Lefkowitz, M. M., & Walder, L. O. (1984). Stability of aggression over time and generations. *Developmental Psychology, 20,* 1120-1134.

Hughes, M. (1998). Turning points in the lives of young inner-city men forgoing destructive criminal behaviors: A qualitative study. *Social Work Research, 22*(3), 143-151.

Huston, A. C., Donnerstein, E., Fairchild, H., Feshbach, N. D., Katz, P. A., Murray, J. P., Rubinstein, E. A., Wilcox, B. L., & Zuckerman, D. (1992). *Big world, small screen: The role of television in American society.* Lincoln, NE: University of Nebraska Press.

Huston, A. C., & Wright, J. C. (1998). Mass media and children's development. In W. Damon (Ed.), *Handbook of child psychology: Vol. 4. Child Psychology in Practice.* (5th ed., pp. 999-1058). New York: Wiley.

Huston, A. C., Wright, J. C., Rice, M. L., Kerkman, D., & St. Peters, M. (1990). Development of television viewing patterns in early childhood: A longitudinal investigation. *Developmental Psychology, 26,* 409-420.

Huston, A. C., Wright, J. C., Wartella, E., Rice, M. L., Watkins, B. A., Campbell, T., & Potts, R. (1981). Communicating more than content: Formal features of children's television programs. *Journal of Communication, 31*(3), 32-48.

Jo, E., & Berkowitz, L. (1994). A priming effect analysis of media influences: An update. In J. Bryant & D. Zillman (Eds.), *Media effects: Advances in theory and research* (pp. 43-60). Hillsdale, NJ: Erlbaum.

Kerkman, D. D., Piñon, M. F., Wright, J. C., & Huston, A. C. (1996). Children's reasoning about video and real balance-scale problems. *Early Education and Development,7,* 237-252.

Koolstra, C. M., & van der Voort, T. H. A. (1996). Longitudinal effects of television on children's leisure-time reading: A test of three explanatory models. *Human Communication Research, 23*(1), 4-35.

Koolstra, C. M., van der Voort, T. H. A., & van der Kamp, L. J. Th. (1997). Television's impact on children's reading comprehension and decoding skills: A 3-year panel study. *Reading Research Quarterly, 32*(2), 128-152.

Kubey, R. W. (1996). Television dependence, diagnosis, and prevention: With commentary on video games, pornography, and media education. In T. M. MacBeth (Ed.), *Tuning in to young viewers* (pp. 221-260). Thousand Oaks, CA: Sage.

Kubey, R., & Csikszentmihalyi, M. (1990). *Television and the quality of life: How viewing shapes everyday experience.* Hillsdale, NJ: Erlbaum.

Kunkel, D. (2001). Children and television advertising. In D. G. Singer & J. L. Singer (Eds.), *Handbook of children and the media* (pp. 375-393). Thousand Oaks, CA: Sage.

Kunkel, D., Cope, K. M., Maynard Farinola, W. J., Biely, E., Rollin, E., & Donnerstein, E. (1999). *Sex on TV.* Menlo Park, CA: Kaiser Family Foundation.

Lefkowitz, M. M., Eron, L. D., Walder, L. O., & Huesmann, L. R. (1972). Television violence and child aggression: A follow-up study. In G. A. Comstock & E. A. Rubinstein (Eds.), *Television and social behavior. Vol. 3: Television and adolescent aggressiveness* (pp. 35-135). Washington, DC: U.S. Government Printing Office.

Leonhardt, D., & Kerwin, K. (1997, June 30). Hey kid, buy this! *Business Week,* 62-67.

Liebert, R. M., & Sprafkin, J. (1988). *The early window: Effects of television on children and youth* (3rd ed.). New York: Pergamon.

Lindlof, T. R., & Meyer, T. P. (1998). Taking the interpretive turn: Qualitative research of television and other electronic media. In J. K. Asamen & G. L. Berry (Eds.), *Research paradigms, television, and social behavior* (pp. 237-268). Thousand Oaks, CA: Sage.

Lovaas, O. I. (1961). Effect of exposure to symbolic aggression on aggressive behavior. *Child Development, 32,* 37-44.

MacBeth, T. M. (1996). Indirect effects of television: Creativity, persistence, school achievement, and participation in other activities. In T. M. MacBeth (Ed.), *Tuning in to young viewers: Social science perspectives on television* (pp. 149-219). Thousand Oaks, CA: Sage.

Maccoby, E. (1951). Television: Its impact on school children. *Public Opinion Quarterly, 15,* 421-444.

Mander, J. (1978). *Four arguments for the elimination of television.* New York: Morrow.

Masters, J. C., Ford, M. E., & Arend, R. A. (1983). Children's strategies for controlling affective responses to aversive social experience. *Motivation and Emotion, 7,* 103-116.

Matthei, H. (1997, May/June). Inventing the commercial. *American Heritage,* 62-68, 70, 72-74.

McGuire, W. J. (1968). Personality and susceptibility to social influence. In E. F. Borgatta & W. W. Lambert (Eds.), *Handbook of personality theory and research* (pp. 1130-1187). Chicago: Rand McNally.

McIntyre, J. J., & Teevan, J. J., Jr. (1972). Television violence and deviant behavior. In G. A. Comstock & E. A. Rubinstein (Eds.), *Television and social behavior. Vol. 3: Television and adolescent aggressiveness* (pp. 383-435). Washington, DC: U. S. Government Printing Office.

McKibben, B. (1992). *The age of missing information.* New York: Random House.

Medrich, E. A., Roizen, J., Rubin, V., & Buckley, S. (1982). *The serious business of growing up: A study of children's lives outside school.* Berkeley, CA: University of California Press.

Miller, M. C. (1988). *Boxed in: The culture of TV.* Evanston, IL: Northwestern University Press.

Minow, N. N. (1995). Introduction. In N. N. Minow & C. L. LaMay, *Abandoned in the wasteland: Children, television, and the First Amendment* (pp. vii-xi). New York: Hill and Wang.

Minow, N. N., & LaMay, C. L. (1995). *Abandoned in the wasteland: Children, television, and the First Amendment.* New York: Hill and Wang.

Molitor, R., & Hirsch, K. W. (1994). Children's toleration of real-life aggression after exposure to media violence: A replication of the Drabman and Thomas studies. *Child Study Journal, 24,* 191-207.

Moore, F. (1999, May 6). Viewers besieged by advertising. *Charleston Post and Courier,* p. 8-D.

Mutz, D. C., Roberts, D. F., & van Vuuren, D. P. (1993). Reconsidering the displacement hypothesis: Television's influence on children's time use. *Communication Research, 20,* 51-75.

National television violence study (Vol. 1). (1997). Thousand Oaks, CA: Sage.

National television violence study (Vol. 2). (1998). Thousand Oaks, CA: Sage.

Neuman, S. B. (1988). The displacement effect: Assessing the relation between television viewing and reading performance. *Reading*

Research Quarterly, 23, 414-440.

Neuman, S. B. (1991). *Literacy in the television age: The myth of the TV effect.* Norwood, NJ: Ablex.

O'Neill Software. (1995). The Text Collector [Computer software]. San Francisco: Author.

Paik, H., & Comstock, G. (1994). The effects of television violence on antisocial behavior: A meta-analysis. *Communication Research, 21,* 516-546.

Parker, E. B. (1963). The effects of television on library circulation. *Public Opinion Quarterly, 27*(4), 578-589.

Pingree, S., & Hawkins, R. (1981). U.S. programs on Australian television: The cultivation effect. *Journal of Communication, 31,* 97-105.

Rice, M. L., Huston, A. C., & Wright, J. C. (1986). Replays as repetitions: Young children's interpretations of television forms. *Journal of Applied Developmental Psychology, 7,* 61-76.

Roberts, E. J. (1982). Television and sexual learning in childhood. In D. Pearl, L. Bouthilet, & J. Lazar (Eds.), *Television and behavior: Ten years of scientific progress and implications for the 80s: Vol. 2. Technical reviews* (pp. 209-223). Washington, DC: U.S. Department of Health and Human Services.

Robinson, J. P. (1972). Television's impact on everyday life: Some cross-national evidence. In E. A. Rubinstein, G. A. Comstock, & J. P. Murray (Eds.), *Television and social behavior: Vol. 4. Television in day-to-day life: Patterns of use* (pp. 410-431). Washington, DC: U.S. Government Printing Office.

Robinson, J. P. (1977). *How Americans use time.* New York: Praeger.

Robinson, J. P. (1981). Television and leisure time: A new scenario. *Journal of Communication, 31,* 120-130.

Rossiter, J. R. (1979). Does television advertising affect children? *Journal of Advertising Research, 19,* 49-53.

Salame, P., & Baddeley, A. (1989). Effects of background music on phonological short-term memory. *The Quarterly Journal of Experimental Psychology, 41A*(1), 107-122.

Salomon, G. (1983). Television watching and mental effort: A social psychological view. In J. Bryant & D. R. Anderson (Eds.), *Children's understanding of television: Research on attention and comprehension* (pp. 181-198). New York: Academic Press.

Salomon, G. (1984). Television is "easy" and print is "tough": The differential investment of mental effort in learning as a function of perceptions and attributions. *Journal of Educational Psychology, 76,* 647-658.

Sapolsky, B. S., & Tabarlet, J. O. (1991). Sex in primetime television: 1979 versus 1989. *Journal of Broadcasting and Electronic Media, 35,* 505-516.

Schramm, W., Lyle, J., & Parker, E. B. (1961). *Television in the lives of our children.* Stanford, CA: Stanford University Press.

Searls, D. T., Mead, N. A., & Ward, B. (1985). The relationship of students' reading skills to TV watching, leisure time reading, and homework. *Journal of Reading, 29,* 158-162.

Shales, T. (1998, July 9). Viewers will tune out lineup. *Charleston Post and Courier,* p. 6-C.

Siegal, M. (1996). Conversation and cognition. In R. Gelman & T. K. Au (Eds.), *Perceptual and cognitive development* (pp. 243-282). San Diego: Academic Press.

Siegler, R. S. (1978). The origins of scientific reasoning. In R. S. Siegler (Ed.), *Children's thinking: What develops?* (pp. 109-149). Hillsdale, NJ: Erlbaum.

Signorielli, N., & Morgan, M. (2001). Television and the family: The cultivation perspective. In J. Bryant & J. A. Bryant (Eds.), *Television and the American family* (2nd ed., pp. 333-351). Mahwah, NJ: Erlbaum.

Singer, D. G. (1993). Creativity of children in a television world. In G. L. Berry & J. K. Asamen (Eds.), *Children and television: Images in a changing sociocultural world* (pp. 73-88). Newbury Park, CA: Sage.

Singer, D. G., & Singer, J. L. (1980). Television viewing and aggressive behavior in preschool children: A field study. In F. Wright, C. Bahn, & R. W. Rieber (Eds.), *Forensic psychology and psychiatry* (Vol. 347, pp. 289-303). New York: The New York Academy of Sciences.

Singer, D. G., & Singer, J. L. (Eds.). (2001). *Handbook of children and the media.* Thousand Oaks, CA: Sage.

Singer, J. L., & Singer, D. G. (1981). *Television, imagination and aggression: A study of preschoolers.* Hillsdale, NJ: Erlbaum.

Singer, J. L., & Singer, D. G. (1983). Implications of childhood television viewing for cognition, imagination, and emotion. In J. Bryant & D. R. Anderson (Eds.), *Children's understanding of television: Research on attention and comprehension* (pp. 265-295). New York: Academic Press.

Steuer, F. B., Applefield, J. M., & Smith, R. (1971). Televised aggression and the interpersonal aggression of preschool children. *Journal of Experimental Child Psychology, 11,* 442-447.

Stone, P. (1986, January/February). TV addiction. *Mother Earth News,* 42-44.

Strasberger, V. C., & Wilson, B. J. (2002). *Children, adolescents, and the media.* Thousand Oaks, CA: Sage.

Strouse, J. S., & Buerkel-Rothfuss, N. L. (1987). Media exposure and the sexual attitudes and behaviors of college students. *Journal of Sex Education and Therapy, 13,* 43-51.

Study finds prime-time ads at record level. (1998, April 29). *The Charleston Post and Courier,* p. 8-B.

Suedfeld, P., Little, B. R., Rank, A. D., Rank, D. S., & Ballard, E. J. (1986). Television and adults: Thinking, personality, and attitudes. In T. M. Williams (Ed.), *The impact of television: A natural experiment in three communities* (pp. 361-394). Orlando, FL: Academic Press.

Sutton-Smith, B. (1997). *The ambiguity of play.* Cambridge, MA: Harvard University Press.

Tan, A. S. (1977). Why TV is missed: A functional analysis. *Journal of Broadcasting, 21,* 371-380.

Television Bureau of Advertising. (2002). Time spent viewing: Per TV home - per day. Retrieved June 4, 2002 from http://www.tvb.org/tvfacts/trends/tv/timespent.html

Thomas, V., & Wolfe, D. B. (1995, May). Why won't television grow up? *American Demographics,* 24-29.

Truglio, R. T., Murphy, K. C., Oppenheimer, S. O., Huston, A. C., & Wright, J. C. (1996). Predictors of children's entertainment television viewing: Why are they tuning in? *Journal of Applied Developmental Psychology, 17,* 475-493.

Tucker, L. A. (1985). Television's role regarding alcohol use among teenagers. *Adolescence, 20,* 593-598.

Tucker, L. A. (1987). Television, teenagers, and health. *Journal of Youth and Adolescence, 16,* 415-425.

U.S. Bureau of the Census. (1994). *Statistical Abstract of the United States: 1994* (114th edition). Washington, DC: U.S. Government Printing Office.

van der Voort, T. H. A., & Valkenburg, P. M. (1994). Television's impact on fantasy play: A review of research. *Developmental Review, 14,* 27-51.

Wilkins, J. A. (1982). *Breaking the TV habit.* New York: Scribners.
Williams, T. M. (Ed.). (1986). *The impact of television: A natural experiment in three communities.* Orlando, FL: Academic Press.
Windahl, S., Höjerback, I., & Hedinsson, E. (1986). Adolescents without television: A study in media deprivation. *Journal of Broadcasting and Electronic Media, 30*(1), 47-63.
Winick, C. (1988). The functions of television: Life without the big box. In S. Oskamp (Ed.), *Television as a social issue* (pp. 217-237). Newbury Park, CA: Sage.
Winn, M. (1985). *The plug-in drug* (Rev. ed.). New York: Penguin.
Wober, J. M. (1990). Never mind the picture, sense the screen. *Journal of Educational Television, 16*(2), 87-93.
Wood, W., Wong, F. Y., & Chachere, J. G. (1991). Effects of media violence on viewers' aggression in unconstrained social interaction. *Psychological Bulletin, 109,* 371-383.
Wright, J. C., Huston, A. C., Ross, R. P., Calvert, S. L., Rolandelli, D., Weeks, L. A., Raeissi, P., & Potts, R. (1984). Pace and continuity of television programs: Effects on children's attention and comprehension. *Developmental Psychology, 20,* 653-666.
Yin, R. K. (1994). *Case study research* (2nd ed.). Thousand Oaks, CA: Sage.
Zuckerman, D. M., Singer, D. G., & Singer, J. L. (1980). Television viewing, children's reading, and related classroom behavior. *Journal of Communication, 30*(1), 166-174.

Author Index

Subject Index

public interest, 88–89

qualitative research. *See* case study method
questionnaires, 4, 5

reading, 4, 6, 7, 8, 9, 10, 11, 13, 20, 21, 22, 26, 27, 67–78, 93, 98–99, 109
background TV, 76, 99
correlational studies, 71–75, 98
reflective thought, 61–62, 64, 97

self-sufficiency. *See* inner resources
sex, 30, 37–39, 39–40, 95–96
effects on viewers, 38–39
prime-time, 38, 83
soap operas, 38

software, Text Collector, 5
spirituality, 7, 93, 97, 100, 101

television addiction. *See* addiction
television as a "substance," 48
television households, 2, 20
thinking. *See* cognition
time, 6, 12, 15–27, 93–94
measuring television use, 16–20
time diary. *See* activity logs
time sharing, 17, 19, 24, 26, 93

"vast wasteland," 89
V-chip, 40
violence. *See* aggression

About the Authors

Faye Steuer has an M.S. degree in Child Development and Family Relationships from Cornell University and a Ph.D. in Psychology from the University of North Carolina at Chapel Hill. She did a postdoctoral fellowship in Pediatric Psychology at the University of Texas Medical Branch at Galveston. She is a professor of psychology at the College of Charleston in Charleston, SC, where she has been teaching since 1976. She is the author of *The Psychological Development of Children* (Brooks/Cole, 1994).

Jason Hustedt holds M.A. and Ph.D. degrees in Developmental Psychology from Cornell University and has completed a postdoctoral fellowship in Urban Education at the University of Pennsylvania's Graduate School of Education. He is currently a research associate at the National Institute for Early Education Research in the Graduate School of Education, Rutgers University, New Brunswick, NJ.